The Journey Through Hallowed Ground

Also by David Edwin Lillard

Appalachian Trail Names (Stackpole, 2002)
Hiking Maryland and Delaware (Falcon, 2006)

OTHER TITLES IN THE CAPITAL
HOMETOWN GUIDES SERIES:

*Dirt Cheap, Real Good: A Highway Guide to Thrift Stores in
the Washington DC Area*
by Chriss Slevin and Leah Smith

*The Middleburg Mystique:
A Peek Inside the Gates of Middleburg, Virginia*
by Vicky Moon

*Quest for the Holy Grill: 50 Crummy but Good
Restaurants within Rambling Range of Washington, DC*
by Donovan Kelly

*The Shopper's Guide to Washington DC:
Where to Find the Best of Everything*
by Karen Ertel and Stephen Koff

*Walk and Bike the Alexandria Heritage Trail:
A Guide to Exploring a Virginia Town's Hidden Past*
by Friends of Alexandria Archaeology (FOAA)

The Journey Through Hallowed Ground

The Official Guide to
Where America Happened™
from Gettysburg to Monticello

David Edwin Lillard

Published with
The Journey Through Hallowed Ground Partnership
www.hallowedground.org

CAPITAL
BOOKS, INC.
Sterling, Virginia

Capital Books, Inc.
P.O. Box 605
Herndon, Virginia 20172-0605

ISBN 10: 1-933102-24-1 (alk. paper)
ISBN 13: 978-1-933102-24-5

Library of Congress Cataloging-in-Publication Data
Lillard, David.
Journey through hallowed ground : a travel guide of heritage sites from Gettysburg to Monticello / David Lillard. — 1st ed.
  p. cm.
ISBN 1-933102-24-1 (alk. paper)
  1. Historic sites—Pennsylvania—Guidebooks. 2. Historic
sites—Maryland—Guidebooks. 3. Historic sites—Virginia—Guidebooks. 4.
Pennsylvania—Tours. 5. Maryland—Tours. 6. Virginia—Tours. 7. United
States Highway 15—Guidebooks. 8. Virginia Route 20 (Va.)—Guidebooks. I.
Title.

F150.L55 2006
917.4804'44—dc22

2006013511

Printed in the United States of America on acid-free paper that meets the American National Standards Institute Z39-48 Standard.

First Edition

10 9 8 7 6 5 4 3 2 1

*The Journey Through Hallowed Ground honors
those whose footprints created and shaped this nation
—from the Susquehannock and Iroquois to Jefferson,
Madison, and Monroe; for those who fought for
freedom and equality.*

*This book is dedicated to the people who protect
the distinctiveness of place: the letter writers, meeting
goers, money raisers, researchers, and entrepreneurs
—those small shop keepers, inn keepers, farmers,
public officials, and Main Street communities.
They too are the Journey.*

Statue at Gettysburg National Military Park. Photo: Katie Lawhon

Monument to the Unknown Soldier at Balls Bluff National Cemetery.
Photo: CMW

Hallowed
Ground

——*Acknowledgments*——

*T*hanks to the Main Street and travel and tourism folks along the Journey for their generosity of time and the introductions they helped make. Thanks also to the staffs and volunteers at the parks, libraries, and sites for all their help. A special thanks to local heritage experts and tour guides who offered insights and ideas, especially Jim Gangawere, Marybeth Mohr, Virginia Morton, and Frank S. Walker, Jr.

Thanks to Cate Magennis Wyatt of The Journey Through Hallowed Ground Partnership for getting me involved in this project; and to Beth Erickson for her help in shaping the manuscript, and Abigail DeLashmutt for her kindness and assistance.

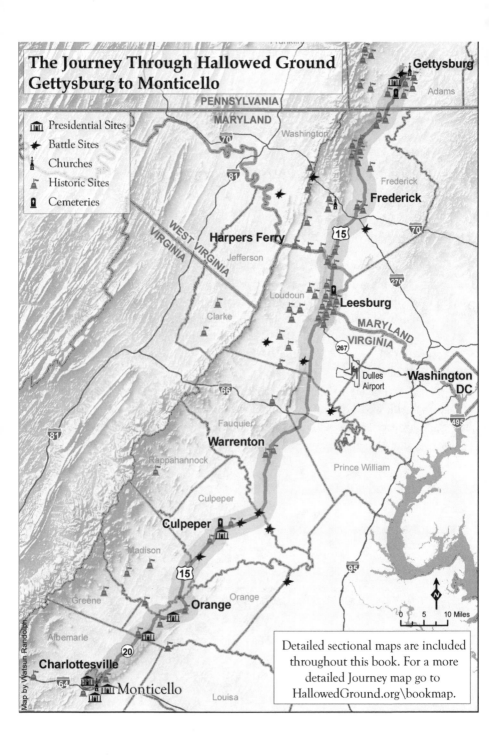

The Journey Through Hallowed Ground
Gettysburg to Monticello

Gettysburg

Adams

PENNSYLVANIA

MARYLAND

Washington

Presidential Sites
Battle Sites
Churches
Historic Sites
Cemeteries

Frederick

Frederick

Harpers Ferry

WEST VIRGINIA

Jefferson

Loudoun

Leesburg

Clarke

MARYLAND
VIRGINIA

Dulles
Airport

**Washington
DC**

Warrenton

Fauquier

Rappahannock

Prince William

Culpeper

Culpeper

Madison

Greene

Orange

Orange

Albemarle

Charlottesville

Monticello

Louisa

0   5   10 Miles

Detailed sectional maps are included
throughout this book. For a more
detailed Journey map go to
HallowedGround.org\bookmap.

Map by Watsun Randolph

Contents

Foreword by Geraldine Brooks   **xiii**
About The Journey Through Hallowed Ground   **xvii**
How to Use This Guide   **xx**
Adams and Frederick Counties Map   **xxiv**

Chapter 1
The Journey Through
Gettysburg to the Potomac River:
Adams County, Pennsylvania and Frederick County, Maryland 1

Travel Assistance   4
Gettysburg   5
    Gettysburg Walking Tours   8
    Historical Sites and Heritage Museums   8
    Eating Out, Hanging Out   13
    Distinctive Shops and Stops   16
    Lodging   17
    To Do Along the Way   18
    Exploring the Countryside   20
Emmitsburg   23
    Historical Sites and Heritage Museums   23
    Eating Out, Hanging Out   25
Thurmont   26
    Historical Sites and Heritage Museums   26
    Eating Out, Hanging Out   28
    Lodging   28
    To Do Along the Way   29
    Exploring the Countryside   30
City of Frederick   30
    Frederick Walking Tours   32
    Historical Sites and Heritage Museums   33
    Eating Out, Hanging Out   37
    Distinctive Shops and Stops   39
    Lodging   41
    To Do Along the Way   42
    Exploring the Countryside   43
Point of Rocks   48
    Historical Sites   49

Chapter **2**

The Journey Through
Loudoun and Prince William Counties, Virginia   53

Loudoun and Prince William Counties Map   52
Travel Assistance   55
From the River to Leesburg   56
Lucketts   57
Leesburg   59
    Tours   60
    Historical Sites and Heritage Museums   62
    Eating Out, Hanging Out   66
    Distinctive Shops and Stops   69
    Lodging   71
    To Do Along the Way   72
    Southern Loudoun   72
    Historical Sites and Heritage Museums   73
    Exploring the Countryside   79
Prince William County   83
    Travel Assistance   83
    Haymarket   84
    Manassas Battlefield Military Park   84
    Old Town Manassas   86

Chapter **3**

The Journey Through
Fauquier and Culpeper Counties, Virginia   89

Fauquier and Culpeper Counties Map   88
Travel Assistance   91
Old Town Warrenton   92
    Warrenton Walking Tour   93
    Historical Sites and Heritage Museums   94
    Eating Out, Hanging Out   98
    Distinctive Shops and Stops   99
    Lodging   101
    Exploring the Countryside   102
Three Battles of the Rappahannock   104
    Historical Sites and Heritage Museums   105
Culpeper   108
    Culpeper Walking Tours   110
    Historical Sites and Heritage Museums   110
    Eating Out, Hanging Out   113

Distinctive Shops and Stops	115
Lodging	117
To Do Along the Way	117
Exploring the Countryside	118

Chapter **4**
The Journey Through
Madison, Orange, and Albemarle Counties, Virginia   123

Madison, Orange, and Albemarle Counties Map	122
Madison County	126
Town of Orange	127
Tours	128
Historical Sites and Heritage Museums	130
Eating Out, Hanging Out	134
Distinctive Shops and Stops	137
Lodging	138
Exploring the Countryside	140
Barboursville	143
Gordonsville	144
James Monroe's Ash Lawn-Highland	145
Monticello	147
Charlottesville	153
Tours	154
Historical Sites and Heritage Museums	154
Eating Out, Hanging Out	156
Distinctive Shops and Stops	158
Lodging	159
To Do in Charlottesville	160
Exploring the Countryside	161

Chapter **5**
Create Your Own Journey:
Scenic Drives to Heritage Sites and Small Towns   165

1. A Presidential Journey with Map	166
2. African American Heritage Tour with Map	176
Harpers Ferry National Historical Park	182
3. Adams County Orchards and Highlands Loop with Map	186
4. Catoctin Scenic Loop with Map	190
5. Potomac Legacy Loop with Map	194
Brunswick	195

6. South Mountain Circuit with Map   201
7. Loudoun-Clarke Scenic Loop   205
      Middleburg   207
      Millwood   213
8. Route 231, Blue Ridge Turnpike Loop   218

Front porch, Waterford, Virginia. Photo: CMW.

——Foreword——
by Geraldine Brooks

*T*he Journey Through Hallowed Ground became my home ground in the most serendipitous way. In 1989, simply wanting to get out of the city on a beautiful early summer morning, we'd set off on an aimless drive. My husband and I were foreign correspondents in those days, working for *The Wall Street Journal* in faraway cities such as Cairo, Sydney, Berlin and London. Back in the United States on a brief home leave, we drove west out of Washington DC, taking small byways, with no plans beyond a picnic lunch by a reach of winding creek somewhere.

Within an hour the city, the suburbs, and the ex-urbs had given way to fields, plowed soft as corduroy or blooming in the urgent green of early corn. The farmhouses and the barns—red, white, weathered gray timbers or miraculous jigsaws of careful drystone —settled gently into the hollows of the landscape, shaded by immense old maples or sycamores. Later, I would learn that one of those huge trees provided an escape route for John Mosby as he climbed out a bedroom window to elude pursuing Union troops. I would come to know that one of the houses we passed had been home to President Monroe. And I would walk fields haunted by the ghosts of missing youths who had died believing deeply in freedom, or in duty.

But that first day I had no idea how dense and how deep the history of this remarkable stretch of ground could be. What captivated me first of all were not links with great figures or great moments of American history, but the remarkable stewardship of land and landscape that had kept the templates of ordinary American lives. When we came over a gentle rise of ground and entered the tiny village of Waterford Virginia, population 250, I was transported by an extraordinary sense of connection with the past.

"Settled in 1733" said a sign at the village edge. Its modest houses, no more than about eighty in all, pressed cozily together, anchored at one end by an old brick grist mill that had once been the settlement's reason for being. The village's footprint had remained small within enfolding pasturelands, grazed by cows and yielding crops as they had for more than two centuries. There were ice houses still standing, evoking a kind of hard, shared, communal toil lost in most contemporary experience. There were root cellars and well pumps that told of a way of life where nothing came without effort, and where the bounty of the earth—its water and its food—could not therefore be wasted in our wanton modern way. The brick church, on the rise of ground near the village's eastern edge, still bore the marks of the shots fired there in a Civil War skirmish. The one room school house built just after that war to educate the village's African American children was a marker on the nation's long and difficult journey towards equality and inclusion. In the cemetery, Union and Confederate dead lay buried side by side in the red clay.

I know that clay now. It is the dirt beneath my fingernails when I come in from tending my garden. Just a few years after that serendipitous summer drive, we moved from London into a small stucco cottage that dated from 1810. I have come to know the place, in the deep and intimate ways you know a place where you begin a family, raise a child. I have learned how to work the same sticky soil that yielded food to the Catoctin Indians who lived here, and the Quakers from Pennsylvania who followed them.

Once a year, during Waterford's annual crafts fair, we open our house for tours, and I love to watch the wonder in the school-children's eyes when I explain to them that the trap door in the kitchen ceiling was where the Quaker children who lived here in the 19th century would be put to bed, hoisted aloft on their parents' shoulders, to sleep in the warm space created by the cooking fire. I let them haul a bucket of water from the stone-lined, hand-dug well, and ask them to imagine how many buckets they would have to haul in a day to cook and bathe and launder for a family. I hand them the Union soldier's belt buckle unearthed near that well, and I see them transported as they turn it in their fingers, trying to imagine the young man who might have worn it. In 1861, many young men in Waterford were Quakers, and therefore pacifists, deeply opposed to all war. But for some, slavery was a greater evil, and so they enlisted to serve on the Union side. I tell the children that maybe the belt buckle belonged to one of those young men, and I watch them frown, and consider his choices, and think about the choice that they would make if they were in his place.

None of this would be possible were it not for the stewardship of the people who lived in this house before us. They valued that old well and the kitchen trap door, and kept them, even though their original purpose had long since become obsolete. They were mindful people who understood that our whims—here, now, this moment—must be measured against an obligation to the past and to the future, which will unfurl into a world whose ways and wants and needs we cannot begin to predict. Because of their stewardship, and the care of hundreds like them, landscapes and buildings still exist in this remarkable region that can tell the story of how and where America happened. They have the power to transport us on the greatest adventure of all: the journey of empathy and imagination into the lives of the people—famous and unknown, humble and distinguished—who shaped this country and made us who we are.

Novelist Geraldine Brooks lives with her writer husband Tony Horwitz and son Nathaniel in Waterford, Virginia, where she found the Union belt buckle that became the inspiration for her second novel, March, *that won the Pulitzer Prize in 2006.*

Spring journey. Photo: Kenneth Garrett

Hallowed
Ground

Gettysburg ★

★ Monticello

——About the Journey
Through Hallowed Ground——

$\mathcal{D}$riving south on The Journey Through Hallowed Ground, along
U.S. Route 15 from Gettysburg, Pennsylvania, it is easy to see why
this stretch of Piedmont leading to Charlottesville, Virginia, means
so much to so many people.

The countryside is lovely and the small towns are charming.
The vistas of the rolling Piedmont and the Blue Ridge Mountains
that border it are pastoral and picturesque. Cows and cattle grazing
on lush pasture have a way of slowing your heart rate and bringing
on smiles. Old town architecture, church steeples, and public
buildings arouse curiosity about the past.

As if the bucolic charm were not enough, at every turn, we are
reminded that the land along the way is significant to our history.
There are Civil War battlefields, presidential homes, and myriad
historic sites that preserve and interpret America's story from the
Colonial period through the Cold War. This truly is "Where America
Happened."

This 175-mile route roughly approximates the way of the Old
Carolina Road, which had been a major migration and trade road
first for the Susquehannock and Iroquois Indians and later for
European settlers. It was home to some of our most notable
American Founders, among them Jefferson, Madison, and Monroe.
It also was a significant corridor during the French and Indian, the
Revolutionary, and Civil wars.

Many of the places along this route are well known to travelers.
Gettysburg, Thomas Jefferson's Monticello, Harper's Ferry, and

Manassas National Battlefield come to mind. Others are just now attaining national and international recognition as destinations, such as Eisenhower National Historic Site, James Madison's Montpelier, and General George Marshall's home, Dodona Manor, in Leesburg.

Then there are the less-known places. Meandering between these historic towns and historic sites that honor both prominent figures and everyday people is like walking through chapters of America's story. There are Underground Railroad sites and sites depicting the Civil Rights movement. There are colonial farmsteads and grand plantation homes. There are more Civil War battlefield sites than any other region in the country, and literally countless sites associated with the Civil War, where we can learn of soldiers and citizens enduring daily hardship that we can only begin to imagine. There are farms that have been in the same family for generations and new farms focusing on organic agriculture.

The region's role in American history is so unquestionably significant that it has been named The Journey Through Hallowed Ground. The name gives you a good idea of how to experience the places along it. The best way to bask in this historic travel route is to travel it yourself. Spend time visiting the historic sites and museums, leisurely wandering the streets of its towns, sampling the cuisine, and taking it all in.

Although The Journey Through Hallowed Ground creates a cohesive story, the places along it have their own distinctive character. Gettysburg, Pennsylvania, and Frederick, Maryland, for example, are barely thirty miles apart; but there is no mistaking one for the other. The same is true for Frederick and Leesburg, Virginia, also about thirty miles apart—and so on down the road. Perhaps what they have most in common is how they pull on visitors to return.

Wherever you go along this Journey, you can see and sense that the landscape is changing. This is most visible, perhaps, among the new houses, shopping areas, and roads. But also recent and expanding are the vineyards, equestrian centers, small-farm and pick-your-own operations, public natural areas, heritage attractions such as steam railroads, and even newly preserved battlefield parks. This changing rural landscape is one that invites the public to enjoy it.

Main Streets have evolved, too. Where they once were places to procure household necessities and farm supplies, they are now places to find fine food, fine art, locally crafted wares, and small luxuries. Former granaries and hardware stores have become coffee shops and galleries. "Country cooking," as often as not, refers to European Provincial cuisine. These, too, are part of change.

These new features on the land have made this region of the Piedmont a wondrous place for travel. You could spend a year of weekends sojourning and still discover new things to see and do. While The Journey Through Hallowed Ground is known as "Where America Happened," it's also where America is happening every day as visitors flock to festivals, shopping, and dining in these historic downtowns.

After you've visited battlefields and historic gardens, you can fly fish or float a lazy river if you want to spend more time outdoors. You can walk from museums to galleries, stopping for lattes and canapés. You'll find hip fashion, high fashion, and high tea. There are wineries and fineries—painted clothing, handmade jewelry, and regional art—bookstores, pottery shops, and of course antiques. And there are delis and dogs—yes, amidst the haute cuisine there are still dogs and kraut, barbecue, fried chicken, and homemade ice cream.

Something you might not notice unless you look for it is the seamless way heritage tourism and commerce work together to create such a pleasing travel experience. In a world of big retail chains, here are the ingenuity and commitment of independent businesses. Through creativity, cooperative ventures, and investment, they have re-invented the Piedmont's small towns while preserving each town's special character.

People who cherish the landscape of The Journey Through Hallowed Ground hope for the same ingenuity and success in the ongoing reinvention of the countryside outside of the Piedmont's small towns, so that changes on the land honor the heritage and celebrate the history.

DAVID LILLARD, MAY 2006

Many people are working to celebrate the special character of the corridor. To that end, they've created a venture known, appropriately enough, as The Journey Through Hallowed Ground Partnership, whose mission is to not only celebrate, conserve, and interpret, for the benefit of residents and visitors alike, this incredible region and its history but also to encourage both Americans and world visitors to Take the Journey™ to appreciate, respect, and experience this cultural landscape that has played an unparalleled role in the creation of America.

You can learn about their efforts by visiting the official website: www.hallowedground.org.

How to Use This Guide

The Journey Through Hallowed Ground is a 175-mile heritage corridor. This guidebook is organized from north to south. Like the Journey itself, it follows U.S. Route 15 south from Gettysburg, Pa. along the Piedmont to Orange, Va., then follows Virginia Route 20/231 through the South-west Mountains into Charlottesville.

The book is divided into five sections. The first four sections describe county-by-county sojourns along the Journey. The fifth section suggests customized itineraries and scenic drives to help you create your own Journey. You can make an adventure of visiting the presidential sites, exploring African American heritage, or finding scenic drives to small towns and mountain vistas.

For the county-by-county sections, there are entries for the historical and heritage sites on and near the Journey. The anchors to the book, as with the Journey, are the small towns that connect the experience. For each town, there is information on touring the sites and visitor services.

📖 WALKING TOURS

Throughout this guidebook, the message is repeated: A guided walk and/or a self-guided brochure are the best ways to get to know these special towns. Nearly all of them have a booklet or map outlining a walk to historic homes and sites. Some have multiple brochures based on themes, such as African American history or the Civil War. Your first stop should be to the visitor center to get one. A listing of visitor centers can be found in each chapter.

Stone walls are a landscape fixture along the Journey.

🏛 HISTORICAL SITES AND HERITAGE MUSEUMS

These entries include sites listed on the National Register of Historic Places, battlefields, and other landmarks that are important to the heritage along The Journey Through Hallowed Ground.

☕ EATING OUT, HANGING OUT

Coffee shops, diners and delis, and full-service restaurants generally are covered in this category. Again, in small towns most establishments are listed. In the larger towns, we can only list enough to entice you to jump in the car and go there.

🎁 DISTINCTIVE SHOPS AND STOPS

These in-town establishments range from galleries and boutiques to museums and grocery stores specializing in local produce. Admittedly, in the smallest towns that have few shops, most or all of the retail businesses of interest to tourists are listed. In the larger towns, it would be impossible to list all the great shops. Frederick and Charlottesville, for example, are among the hippest small

Photo: CMW

cities in America. For a guide of this focus, the best strategy is to offer a sampling of what might whet your appetite for a visit.

LODGING

With a few exceptions, these entries focus on in-town, independently owned bed and breakfasts or country inns. In towns without many B&B offerings, the listings include inns and B&Bs nearby.

🚗 TO DO ALONG THE WAY

A grab bag of activities, from hot-air balloons to steam trains and ghost walks.

🌲 EXPLORING THE COUNTRYSIDE

There is so much to see and do within close proximity to The Journey Through Hallowed Ground. These entries are countryside junkets from the small towns covered in the guidebook. They include:

- ✧ Heritage sites nearby
- ✧ Farms and wineries
- ✧ Outdoor recreation
- ✧ Villages and small towns

Photo: Mike DeHart

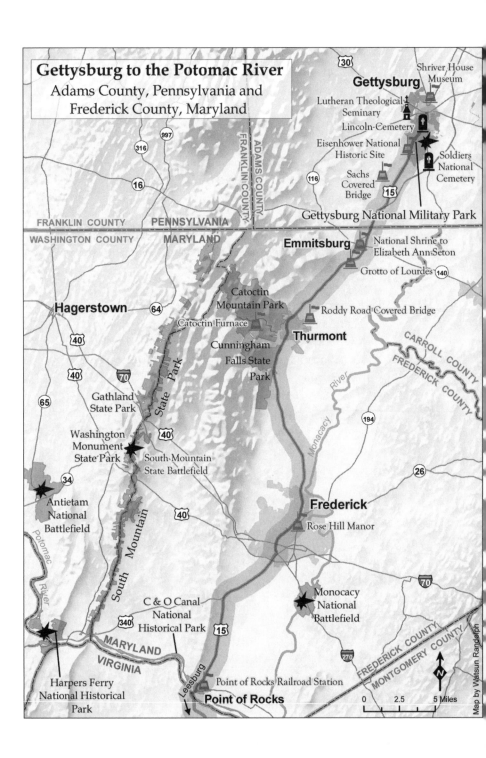

Gettysburg to the Potomac River
Adams County, Pennsylvania and
Frederick County, Maryland

30

Gettysburg

Shriver House Museum

Lutheran Theological Seminary

Lincoln Cemetery

Eisenhower National Historic Site

Soldiers National Cemetery

Sachs Covered Bridge

15

Gettysburg National Military Park

116

316

997

FRANKLIN COUNTY

ADAMS COUNTY

FRANKLIN COUNTY   PENNSYLVANIA

WASHINGTON COUNTY   MARYLAND

16

Emmitsburg

National Shrine to Elizabeth Ann Seton

Grotto of Lourdes 140

Catoctin Mountain Park

Catoctin Furnace

Roddy Road Covered Bridge

Hagerstown   64

Thurmont

CARROLL COUNTY

FREDERICK COUNTY

Cunningham Falls State Park

Monocacy River

40

40

70

State Park

194

65

Gathland State Park

Washington Monument State Park   40

South Mountain State Battlefield

Frederick

26

34

40

Rose Hill Manor

Antietam National Battlefield

South Mountain

70

Potomac River

C & O Canal National Historical Park

340

15

Monocacy National Battlefield

270

MARYLAND

VIRGINIA

Leesburg

Point of Rocks Railroad Station

FREDERICK COUNTY

MONTGOMERY COUNTY

Harpers Ferry National Historical Park

Point of Rocks

N

0   2.5   5 Miles

Map by Watsun Randolph

Chapter 1

The Journey Through
Gettysburg to the Potomac River: Adams County, Pennsylvania and Frederick County, Maryland

Distance: 46 MILES

HIGHLIGHTS ALONG THE JOURNEY THROUGH HALLOWED GROUND

Miles	Site
START	GETTYSBURG
14	EMMITSBURG, SHRINE TO ELIZABETH ANN SETON
15	GROTTO OF LOURDES
18	RODDY CREEK ROAD TO RODDY COVERED BRIDGE
19	MAIN STREET THURMONT
19.5	CATOCTIN FURNACE
34	ROSE HILL MANOR
35	HISTORIC DOWNTOWN FREDERICK
48	POINT OF ROCKS

Gettysburg is the northern end of The Journey Through Hallowed Ground. Stretching south from here, U.S. Route 15 roughly traces a pathway that has been a trade and migration route for centuries. In the heyday of the frontier, German and Scots-Irish colonists came from Philadelphia at a rate of thousands each year, some

The Virginia Monument, Gettysburg National Military Park.
Photo: Steven L. Spring

stopping to settle the area that is now Adams County, Pa., and Frederick County, Md. Others, many more, continued south across the Potomac River into Loudoun and neighboring counties east and west of the Blue Ridge.

There was a time when a trip to Gettysburg meant one thing: a morning touring Gettysburg National Battlefield followed by an afternoon in pursuit of Civil War memorabilia in the shops lining the road into downtown. And if that is the extent of your desires, you can still find it. No worries there. In fact, a new battlefield visitor center, scheduled to open in 2007, will bring new interpretations and new exhibits. Beyond the battlefield, Gettysburg the town has its own appeal: galleries, performances, poetry readings, as well as attractions tied to its heritage as a historic small town.

Like other Piedmont counties, Adams is bordered to the west by mountains. South Mountain, sometimes called the South Mountains, is the northern tip of the Blue Ridge, which is a constant companion when traveling The Journey Through Hallowed Ground to Charlottesville.

From the bluffs above Gettysburg, the mountains appear as a backdrop for a pastoral painting. Approaching the ridge is a different story. The roads narrow and become tree lined, the temperature drops, and the visitor orientation turns to mountain recreation. If you stay an extra day, you will have time to hike the Appalachian Trail and enjoy the scenic vistas from Micheaux State Forest, returning to Gettysburg in time for battlefield sunsets, dinner and ghost walks, or strolls to your favorite Gettysburg haunts.

The scenic way to start the Journey is to travel through the battlefield south on Business Route 15, which you can follow into Frederick County and the town of Emmitsburg. Traveling south from Emmitsburg there are lovely views of the Catoctin Mountain ridgeline all the way to Frederick City. Along that ridgeline is a chain of parkland stretching twenty miles, connecting one national park, two state parks, and a municipal forest.

Active settlement in Frederick County began in 1732 when a few families purchased huge tracts of land, ranging from several thousand to tens of thousands of acres. Their names, Calvert, Carroll, Johnson, and Dulaney are represented on dozens of place names and landmarks today. At that time, German settlers began purchasing smaller parcels and forming settlements in the eastern and central parts of the county, while Scots-Irish highlanders settled

in the western mountains. The brisk traffic and trade they created along the Pied-mont from Southern Pennsylvania to the Virginia Piedmont continues today along Route 15.

The county seat and cultural hub, the City of Frederick, is a wonderful little city with a stylish air that does not overwhelm

A roadside stand along Adams County's 30,000 acre Fruit Belt.
Photo: CMW

its friendliness. As Maryland's second largest city, it has played an important role in history. It was the home of the first president of the Constitutional Convention, Maryland's first elected governor, and the meeting place for the state legislature while it debated secession in 1861.

Four years later, just southeast of town was fought the "Battle That Saved Washington," a battle that many historians say altered the course of the Civil War. The site of the battle is preserved as Monocacy National Battlefield.

South of the City of Frederick, the area near the Potomac River is among the most significant places in American history for three transportation stories. The Chesapeake & Ohio Canal National Historical Park is the best-preserved example of the American canal

TRAVEL ASSISTANCE

Gettysburg Convention and Visitors Bureau
Stop by for area maps and brochures.
102 Carlisle St.;
(800) 337-5015;
www.gettysburgcvb.org.

Main Street Gettsyburg
(717) 337 3491;
www.mainstreetgettysburg.org.

Tourism Council of Frederick County
Visitor center at
19 East Church St., in Frederick;
(301) 644-4047;
www.fredericktoursim.org.

Downtown Frederick Partnership
Information about upcoming events, including the monthly gallery walk.
(301) 698-8118
www.downtownfrederick.org.

era; the 184-mile park and trail follows the Potomac shoreline west through Frederick County. The Baltimore & Ohio was the first long-haul rail line in the country; it parallels the canal through the county. And Frederick was a key passage in a railway of a different sort—the Underground Railroad.

Gettysburg

For veteran visitors, there's a "hey, that's new!" sense of discovery even while you're getting that comforting feeling of a familiar small town. You will notice the first improvement as soon as you start strolling the sidewalks—wayside markers placed throughout the downtown area. Set in front of private homes, churches, businesses, schools, and other vintage structures, the markers tell the story of Gettysburg from the point of view of the people who have lived there.

To be sure, the primary storyline is the Battle of Gettysburg, but your perspective is enlarged. Through personal stories, you see a little town in the midst of war whose fabric was every bit as complex as the nation as a whole. Officially committed to the Union, Adams County was nevertheless linked economically to the South via the Carolina Road, now U.S. 15. You discover a place where the pressing national issues of the day, such as free public education, slavery, and the role of the federal government, were as charged and tenuous as they were in any place in America. As a result, just while meandering through Gettysburg to fawn over charming old buildings, you learn a lot about the America that dissolved into the Civil War in 1861.

You also see the battle in a new way. For the first time, it becomes a house-to-house street fight. Soldiers are shot on doorsteps as they bang on doors desperately seeking refuge; they are picked off in alleys by rooftop snipers. Residents cower in cellars to stay clear of stray bullets. It's a very different battle than the one best known for its half-mile formation lines and cornfield charges.

You can follow them in an ordered, self-guided walking tour described on a pocket map of the town. Or, you can happen upon

Remembrance Day in Gettyburg National Military Park.
Photo: Kenneth Garrett

the markers randomly while sidling window to window to preview restaurant menus or walking off those Adams County staples, a hot dog and milkshake—thank goodness some things don't change!

You can take a break from the Civil War altogether and still have lots to do in Gettysburg. There are galleries, pubs, eateries, and music. With the restoration of the Majestic Theater, a block from Lincoln Square, there are nationally known acts and touring companies passing through each week.

The secret of Gettysburg that eludes many travelers is that it's a great place to just hang out. Understandably, with so much history and so many attractions, you want to see it all. But sitting in Lincoln Square, reading some local history while nibbling on a treat no cardiologist would ever recommend, that's nice, too. Then, pull yourself onto your feet and walk a block to the train station for a scenic railroad tour of the countryside.

Following that, walk the town, the historic college campus, or the Seminary grounds. The best way to experience Gettysburg is on foot on a guided walking tour. Better yet, hire one of Main Street Gettysburg's licensed town guides for a personalized tour. Because Gettysburg is a borough full of legends, getting a licensed guide is the best way to separate the folklore from the history.

Lutheran Theological Seminary, founded in 1826, is the oldest continuing Lutheran seminary in America. Photo: Steven L. Spring

For a town that gets more than two million visitors a year, Gettysburg is an unexpectedly affordable place to stay, with deluxe B&B rooms priced about the same as a budget hotel in a larger city. For budget travelers, most of the B&Bs have rooms that run the gamut on price.

📖 GETTYSBURG WALKING TOURS

BATTLEFIELD GUIDES.
Association of Licensed Battlefield Guides; www.gettysburgtourguides.org.

DOWNTOWN WALKING TOURS.
Main Street Gettysburg; (717) 337-3491; www.mainstreetgettysburg.org/guidedtour.

🏛 HISTORICAL SITES AND HERITAGE MUSEUMS

Eisenhower National Historic Site

President and Mrs. Eisenhower purchased the farm in 1950 as a weekend retreat. Adjacent to the battlefield, the farm would become their permanent home after his presidency. As a career military man, this was the only home the couple ever owned. The homestead sits in a magnificent setting, with views stretching to South Mountain. Eisenhower shunned fancy surroundings, having had his fill at the White House. Reflecting his personal taste, the house is a kind of 1950s informal—remember, this is an era in which many men wore ties on the weekends! It is presented largely the way Ike and Mamie lived there. On the porch (his favorite room), you find an easel with one of his unfinished paintings, shelves full of Mamie's favorite books (including one by Stephen King), and the television where Ike never tired of watching "I Love Lucy." Note there is no parking at the site. Access to the Eisenhower Farm is by shuttle

The Eisenhower homestead sits in a magnificent setting with views stretching to South Mountain. Photo: Steven L. Spring

bus from the Gettysburg Battlefield Visitor Center only. To visit the Eisenhower Farm, purchase a ticket at the battlefield visitor center, 97 Taneytown Rd. Eisenhower National Historic Site open daily, 9 to 4.

Gettysburg National Military Park

The battlefield at Gettysburg ranks among the most famous, most visited places in America. And yet, you can almost always find solitude amid the memorials and storied locations—especially if you're able to visit midweek. It is a battle in which the chronicles of privates and corporals have endured alongside generals and politicians. Every visit reveals a new story of some small detail that in its way adds to the drama of battle. Add to that the setting of the battlefield. Were no battle ever fought here, the park could still be considered among the most scenic places a traveler could find.

Gettysburg National Military Park.
Photo: Katie Lawhon

Here are a few recommendations to make the most of your visit. First, stay for more than a day. You have to make time to find a quiet corner and imagine. Second, to help your imaginings, get a battlefield guide. The licensed guides hired at the visitor center set the standard by which all park interpreters should be judged. If you take the two-hour guided tour first, you can go back to your favorite spots. You can even take tours on horseback. Finally, take some time to walk the Civil War circuit in town and visit other sites of the battle, such as Brenners Hill.

Park grounds and roads open daily, 6 a.m. to 10 p.m., April through October; and until 7 p.m., November through March. The visitor center is open daily, 8 to 5. (6 p.m. in summer). Camping (yes—camping on the battlefield!) is available to organized youth groups at the McMillan Woods Youth Campground; consult the park website or call.

Reenactor at the Gettysburg National Military Park, Remembrance Day, November 19, 2005. Photo: Kenneth Garrett

Lincoln Cemetery

An organization of African American men called the Sons of Good Will established the cemetery in 1867 for the burial of Gettysburg's black Civil War veterans, who were denied burial in the National Cemetery. Thirty Civil War veterans are buried here. In 1906, when housing development uprooted the town's other black cemetery, the remains were transferred here and the cemetery renamed Lincoln Cemetery. Long Lane, Gettysburg. From Baltimore Street, west on Breckenridge, left on Long Lane. www.brotherswar.com/These_Honored_Dead-7c.htm.

Soldiers' National Cemetery

Across from the battlefield visitor center, this peaceful knoll overlooking the town is where Abraham Lincoln delivered the Gettysburg Address in 1863. The cemetery came about of necessity. Thousands of soldiers who died at Gettysburg had been hastily buried in shallow graves in scattered fields, there awaiting final burial. A group of Gettysburg citizens, with assistance from Pennsylvania, founded and funded the purchase of the land and the re-interment of the soldiers. Soldiers' National Monument stands at the center of the cemetery. The text of Lincoln's speech is transcribed on a plaque at a memorial. Veterans of all major U.S. conflicts are buried here. Open daily, dawn till sunset. www.nps.gov/gett/gncem.htm.

Rupp House History Center

A project of the Friends of National Parks at Gettysburg, Rupp House History Center presents interactive displays depicting nineteenth century life and culture, stories of Civil War soldiers, and the impact of the war on local families. Open daily March through October. 451 Baltimore St.; 717-334-7292; www.friendsofgettysburg.org.

Shriver House Museum

This unique museum focuses exclusively on the civilian experience during the Civil War, particularly the Battle of Gettysburg via the perspective of the Shriver family. You also learn about American life during the war and the years preceding it. The Shriver home was new at the time of the battle, having been completed in 1860. In addition to serving as the Shriver home, the building housed a taproom and bowling alley. After decades of decay, the property has been purchased and restored by a private foundation. Thirty-minute guided tours of the Shriver House are conducted every half-hour. Note: You might see the name spelled "Schriver" in older publications. Daily, April through November. Weekends only, December, February, and March. 309 Baltimore St.; www.shriverhouse.org.

Wills House

Yes, Lincoln really did sleep here. This three-story brick Federal is the home where President Lincoln stayed on the occasion of his cemetery dedication address. It was built about 1816 as a commercial building for merchant Alexander Cobean, a founder of Adams County. David Wills purchased it in 1859. It was his invitation to Lincoln that led to the president's attendance at the cemetery's dedication and Lincoln's now famous speech. In 2004, the National Park Service purchased the Wills House for a museum, which is scheduled to open in 2007. www.emmitsburg.net/achs/articles/property/wills_house.htm).

☕ EATING OUT, HANGING OUT

Avenue Restaurant. This family-style restaurant is a Gettysburg tradition; good homemade food in an immaculate dining room. 21 Steinwehr Ave.; (717) 334-3235.

Dobbin House Colonial Tavern and Inn.
Photo: Steven L. Spring

Blue Parrot Bistro. Understated and comfortably hip, with a bar in front and a single pool table between the bar and dining room, which is lined on both sides with booths. For lunch, a variety of soups, sandwiches, and salads—the chicken souvlaki salad is a yummy garlicky pile of food. Dinner entrees include vegetarian selections. Music at night. 35 Chambersburg St.; (717) 337-3739.

Cashtown Inn, Cashtown, Pa. This inn has served travelers since 1797. It was Gettysburg headquarters for Confederate General A.P. Hill. There are gardens to stroll and a porch for sitting. Closed Mondays, reservation advised for dinner. (717) 334-9722; www.cashtowninn.com.

Dobbin House. This Colonial tavern and inn offers dining and lodging in the oldest building in Gettysburg. Its museum quality woodworking and original fireplaces alone are enough to recommend it. Unlike museums that interpret Colonial America, you can eat, drink, and lodge here. Eat downstairs in the Springhouse Tavern, and check out the Underground Railroad exhibit upstairs. 89 Steinwehr Ave.; (717) 334-2100; www.dobbinhouse.com.

Ernie's Texas Lunch. When a patron asks for one with everything to go, you know they're talkin' hotdogs. Get one just for walking around town. For a real treat, sit at the counter for some soup. Open daily for lunch. 58 Chambersburg St.; (717) 334-1970.

Farnsworth House. The tavern and dining room are both among Gettysburg's most popular spots. The game pie is a contemporary version of a nineteenth-century classic. Showing complete neutrality between North and South, both Yankee pot roast and the Virginia ham with crab cake are on the menu. 401 Baltimore St.; (717) 334-8838; www.farnsworthhouseinn.com.

O'Rourke's. Wooden booths, a beautiful bar, acoustic music at
night, good food, one tastefully placed television for
watching a game . . . what more needs to be said?
44 Steinwehr Ave.; (717) 334-2333.

Ragged Edge Coffee House. A fine place to hang and read,
serving coffee, teas, and fresh-squeezed juices. The menu
includes sandwiches, salads, bagels, and an especially diverse
array for the vegetarian-inclined; soups too. Good fresh
food, music at night. 110 Chambersburg St.;
(717) 334-4464; www.raggededgecoffeehs.com.

✠ DISTINCTIVE SHOPS AND STOPS

Artworks. Creative home décor and interior accessories. 42 York
St.; (717) 334-4250.

Book Cellar. Five rooms of used, antiquarian, and out-of-print
books in a delightfully claustrophobic space. One of the
Journey's great bookstores. Closed Tuesdays and
Wednesdays, open Thursdays for a couple of hours, and,
well, you get the picture. 22 Carlisle St.; half a block north
of Lincoln Square; (717) 337-0557.

Gallery 30. A metaphor-defying shop, this is a bookstore and gallery
dealing in fine arts, handmade jewelry, and pottery—all of
it first rate. As if that weren't enough, there also is an
extensive collection of children's books and kid-oriented
art. 30 York St.; (717) 334-0335; www.gallery30.com.

Homefront 40's. Home décor, gifts, and domestic accessories with
an eye toward the nostalgic mid-twentieth century.
25 York St.; (717) 337-3741.

Just Jennifer. The very definition of eclectic, the shop deals in
original artwork in such diverse media as paintings, pottery,

brass sculpture, glassware, and handcrafted and Native American jewelry. And just for the "why not?" factor, there are spa and bath products, gourmet foods, and an array of stuff that somehow all seems to make sense under the same roof. 33 York St.; (717) 338-9099; www.justjennifergallery.com.

Lord Nelson's Nature Store and Gallery. A fantastic find, in a Civil War town no less, Lord Nelson's is known as the leading exhibitor of American frontier art, especially from the French and Indian War period. The gallery has a unique collection of books and maps covering the frontier era, as well. There is also an extensive offering of wildlife and handcrafted art. Open daily. 27 1/2 Chambersburg St.; (717) 334-7950.

Majestic Theater. After undergoing major restorations, this grand old theater has rediscovered its glory days. Movies on the big (big!) screen, plays, and music are the fare at this Gettysburg landmark, which in the 1950s regularly hosted President and Mrs. Eisenhower while they were at their home in Gettysburg. In addition to the touring performances, a Civil War musical called *For the Glory* plays during summer. 25 Carlisle St.; (717) 337-8200; www.gettysburgmajestic.org.

🛏 LODGING

Battlefield Bed & Breakfast. Just outside of town on a thirty-acre farm, the original house was built in 1809. The kid-friendly inn has lots of common space for guests, including a great room. Each morning starts with a short history presentation. There are special weekends for ghost stories, mystery theater, and packages with local restaurants. 2264 Emmitsburg Rd.; (717) 334-8804; www.gettysburgbattlefield.com.

Brafferton Inn. Built in 1786 and located a half block from Lincoln Square, the Codori House is the oldest continual residence in Gettysburg. It's an elegant place but still family friendly. There are a number of suites with adjoining sitting rooms. The third-floor loft suite has exposed stone walls and rafters. 44 York St.; (717) 337-3423; www.brafferton.com.

Brick House Inn. Less than a block from the battlefield, this 1898 Victorian has eight guest rooms; there are four more in the adjacent Welty House, which dates to 1830. In summer, have breakfast, complete with shoofly pie, on the patio out back. Kids welcome. 452 Baltimore St.; (717) 338-9337; www.brickhouseinn.com.

The Gaslight Inn. The inn has nine charming rooms, comfortable sitting rooms, a welcoming porch, and a quiet patio out back. Many of the rooms have fireplaces. The innkeepers and staff know the region well and love to share their favorites with guests. The inn bills itself as an in-town oasis; the moniker would be hard to dispute. 33 East Middle St.; (717) 337-9100; www.thegaslightinn.com.

James Gettys Hotel. A classic and distinguished small hotel, the Gettys is listed on the National Register of Historic Places. Continental breakfast is served in your room; kids under twelve stay free. The hotel is a half block from Lincoln Square. 27 Chambersburg St.; (800) 900-5275; www.jamesgettyshotel.com.

🚗 To Do Along the Way

Boyds Bear Country. You're on vacation; it's raining. It's time to tour a teddy bear factory, store, and museum. It's big and little kids love it. A few miles south of Gettysburg on

Sach's Bridge, built in 1852. Imagine the caissons and cannon rumbling over the wooden planks. Photo: Steven L. Spring

Cunningham Road (you'll see the signs). Open Thursday through Monday, 10 to 6.

Ghost Tours. There several ghost tour outfits; some getting higher marks than others. Here are two that come recommended:

■ **Farnsworth House**, Gettysburg. A one-hour presentation down the dark stone stairway into the funeral parlor, or follow guides in period dress as they lead you through darkened streets. (717) 334-8838; www.farnsworthhouseinn.com.

■ **Ghosts of Gettysburg**. Tour based on the best-selling books by Gettysburg author and ghost-guy Mark Nesbitt. (717) 337-0445; www.ghostsofgettysburg.com.

Have a picnic at a Covered Bridge. Sach's Covered Bridge, on Pumping Station Road near Gettysburg. Follow Pumping Station Road from Confederate Avenue on the battlefield; just after crossing Marsh Creek, turn left onto Scotts Road and go about two hundred yards to the bridge parking area. Built in 1852, Sach's Bridge is more than a charming artifact. Standing on the bridge, you can imagine the caissons and cannon rumbling over the wooden planks. The bridge was preserved by the Gettysburg Battlefield Preservation Association and is on the National Register of Historic Places. www.gbpa.org.

Ride the Scenic Railroad. Choose from a scenic ride with narration as you pass through Civil War-related sites, or a nighttime ghost train, or a dinner aboard the train while enjoying the sounds of big band music. See the website for schedules. Reservations suggested. 106 N. Washington St., Gettysburg; (717) 334-6932; www.gettysburgrail.com.

See the Battlefield on Horseback. Many people don't realize there is a network of nicely groomed hiker-equestrian trails through the battlefield. You can take a one- to four-hour ride and see the land the way the soldiers saw it. No kid will ever forget this experience; not a bad idea for a date, either. Minimum age is eight. Hickory Hollow Farm; (717) 334-0349; www.hickoryhollowfarm.com.

Stop and Shop at an Orchard Market. Along the thirty-thousand-acre Fruit Belt are roadside stands selling fresh Adams County apples, peaches, berries, plums, and more.

EXPLORING THE COUNTRYSIDE

Wineries and Farms

Adams County Winery, Ortanna, Pa. Located at the end of a country lane, the winery is a scenic spot for a tasting and a picnic. Chambourcin wines, which fare well in the Mid–Atlantic, are the featured variety, but there is much to sample and enjoy, including a number of fruity semi-sweets. This is a friendly, informal place to learn about wines of the region. You can purchase snacks for a fancy picnic under the pines. (717) 334-4631; www.adamscountywinery.com.

The Historic Round Barn, Cashtown, Pa. This architectural marvel was built at the height of the round barn era in 1914. Now owned by Knouse Fruitlands, the barn is a market for a huge variety of fruits, berries, and vegetables, and an assortment of jams and other farm bounty. Stop by in autumn for cider pressing. Kids enjoy the farm animals outside. Men just like looking at the barn. (717) 334-1984; www.roundbarngettysburg.com.

Outdoor Recreation

Battlefield on Bicycle or Foot. Taking a hike or ride doesn't have to mean heading to the mountains. Bicycling is the most pleasing way to travel the park roads, and covering some of the key ground on foot gives you the best sense of the terrain.

Strawberry Hill Preserve, Fairfield, Pa. More than six hundred acres of mountain streams below Mount Hope. Enjoy a stroll by Middle Creek or take a walk on the wide, gently graded paths. Picnic tables and exhibits. www.strawberryhill.org.

Small Towns near Gettysburg

Fairfield. This one-street town, eight miles west of Gettysburg on Route 116, is a favorite for hikers and families vacationing in Micheaux State Forest and Pine Grove Furnace State

Park. They come down out of the mountains in search of comestibles just as Robert E. Lee's men did on their retreat from Gettysburg. Fairfield offers a pleasant lunch detour while on the Scenic Valley Driving Tour (see Scenic Drives). For a casual lunch, on the east end of town there is the Village Table Diner (yep, it's a real diner) and Ventura's Pizzeria. On the west end is tiny Q's Cup, for sandwiches, soup, and coffee.

Or stop in at the Historic Fairfield Inn. This tavern has been serving up ale since 1757. Its patrons have included Patrick Henry, Robert E. Lee, and President and Mrs. Eisenhower. There is a tavern for casual dining and spirits, and an elegant dining room. How's this for entertainment? Your party can order up a Civil War-era dinner theater presentation in a private room upstairs. (717) 334-8868; www.thefairfieldinn.com.

New Oxford. A stop on the Conegwego Scenic Tour, ten miles east of Gettysburg (see Scenic Drives), New Oxford is an antique shoppers Mecca. The town is an architectural gem with an attractive central square, worthy of a leg-stretching walk if you're on the driving tour. New Oxford's main event is the annual Christmas home tour, second Saturday in December.

———

Driving south through the battlefield, there are winter views west of the Eisenhower Farm and South Mountain. Further on, you will pass a couple of less-visited battlefield sites, where you might be more likely to share a field with songbirds than people. At the junction with Route 15's main artery, you can continue on this two-lane road, which winds its way to Emmitsburg and crosses the main road again just north of town.

Emmitsburg, a tiny town with a charming Main Street.
Photo: Steven L. Spring

Emmitsburg

Emmitsburg is a tiny town with a charming Main Street. Once a bustling town in the middle of one of America's most productive wheat-producing regions, it is best known now for two attractions: the Grotto of Lourdes and the National Shrine of Elizabeth Ann Seton. The town was chartered in 1785 as a remote outpost for Catholic Maryland. Before and after the Battle of Gettysburg, the fields surrounding the town were the site of massive Union encampments. One of its principle assets today is its lovely setting beneath the Catoctins, which you can enjoy during a stroll down Main Street to admire the architecture. Emmitsburg is also the home of the National Fallen Firefighters Memorial.

🏛 HISTORICAL SITES AND HERITAGE MUSEUMS

National Shrine of Elizabeth Ann Seton

Among American Catholics, Frederick County is best known as the home of Elizabeth Ann Seton, the first

National Shrine of Elizabeth Ann Seton, the first American-born person to be canonized a saint. Photo: Steven L. Spring

American-born person to be canonized a saint. Here, after her husband's death, she, her sisters-in-law, and other Sisters of Charity tended the needs of widowed mothers and ran a school for girls from 1809 until her death in 1821. The historic sites on the property include the Stone House, occupied 1809-10; the White House, a stately two-story cabin covered in clapboard that became the main house and school; and the Old Cemetery. Surrounded by a stone wall, the cemetery is a lovely, peaceful spot with row upon row of simple white stone markers. Whatever your religious persuasion, the shrine is an essential stop along The Journey Through Hallowed Ground. Tuesday through Sunday, 10 to 4:30. www.emmitsburg.net/setonshrine.

Grotto of Lourdes

This peaceful garden above Mount St. Mary's University draws Catholic visitors worldwide. It began as a simple cross in a hillside grotto in the early nineteenth century.

Not long after, paths and landscaping created a formal place for reflection. Decades later, a shrine was created here in honor of the Lady at the Grotto of Massabielle, also known as the Lady of Lourdes.

National Fallen Firefighters Memorial

On the grounds of the National Fire Academy, the memorial honors career and volunteer firefighters who have died in duty. The centerpiece of the monument is a bronze Maltese cross atop a seven-foot stone cairn. The cross is replicated in the shape of the grounds surrounding the memorial, where plaques list the names of the firefighters killed in service since 1981. 16825 S. Seton Ave.; www.usfa.fema.gov/fatalities/memorial.

⚕ Eating Out, Hanging Out

Carriage House Inn. Comfortable dining in a nineteenth century building, with seafood featured at lunch (go for the crab cake) and American fare at dinner. 200 S. Seton Ave.; (301) 447-2366; www.carriagehouseinn.info.

Chubby's Southern Style Barbecue. Sitting at the counter or table, Chubby's evokes that old roadhouse feel. The smoky ribs, cooked over oak and hickory coals, beckon harried travelers to the take-out window, but the way those sandwiches are stuffed it's a traffic hazard. The real deal. Open daily. Route 15 and Old Frederick Rd.; (301) 447-3322.

Ott House Pub. A pub serving casual fare and libations to locals, this laid-back place features dartboards, pool tables, and sports on the tube. Live music from classic rock to Motown, and a dance floor too. Open daily. 5 W. Main St.; (301) 447-2625.

The Palms. Full-service American fare and cocktails. (301) 447-3689; 1620 W. Main St.

Stavarus Pizza. It's where the college crowd goes for eats, and arcade video games. Pizza and sandwiches. 2 E. Main St.; (301) 447-6767.

Whether you travel the side roads or Route 15, there are two stops north of Thurmont. The first is **Catoctin Mountain Orchard** for pick-your-own or something from the market (see listing under To Do Along the Way, Thurmont) The second is **Roddy Covered Bridge** (take Roddy Creek Road exit, and go about a half mile). There are picnic tables at the bridge if you want to snack on those berries from the market. Retrace your route almost back to Route 15 and turn left on Route 806, which leads to Thurmont.

Thurmont

This tiny village's sleepy streets come alive for the annual Catoctin Colorfest, the area's largest juried crafts show. During summer months, Thurmont is a popular place for vacationers from Cunningham Falls and Catoctin Mountain parks to come in to town for dinner. Any time of year, it's a nice place to get out of the car and stroll Water and Main streets.

🏛 HISTORICAL SITES AND HERITAGE MUSEUMS

Catoctin Furnace

The furnace historic site is just south of Thurmont, following Frederick Road, which becomes Catoctin Furnace Road. Gazing at the quilt work of the Catoctin

Mountains autumn colors, it's hard to imagine that the surrounding forest was once denuded of hardwoods to make charcoal. Over nearly one hundred years of firing Catoctin Furnace with charcoal, its owners cleared eleven thousand acres beginning in 1776. More than three hundred woodcutters were employed to give colliers a steady supply to make charcoal. When operations ceased in 1903, the furnace's usable parts were sold for use at other foundries. In 1936, the federal government purchased ten thousand acres as recreation land and to demonstrate forest restoration. Today, Catoctin Furnace is part of Cunningham Falls State Park.

You can hike over from the park, or enjoy a brief rest stop when traveling Route 15 (take Catoctin Furnace exit). Open daily.

www.dnr.state.md.us/publiclands/cunninghamguide.html.

Catoctin Furnace operated from 1776 to 1903, making iron.
Photo: Steven L. Spring

♨ EATING OUT, HANGING OUT

Cozy Restaurant. The Cozy is Americana and has been since 1929. The haunt of White House staffs and press corps when the President is at nearby Camp David, the restaurant has a very fine Camp David Museum adjacent to its notable barroom. There are shops and lodging as well. 103 Frederick Rd. (Rt. 806); (301) 271-4301; www.cozyvillage.com.

Kountry Kitchen. Real country food and real country prices; where the locals eat. A kids' menu and a full bar round it out. Open for breakfast, lunch, and dinner. 17 Water St.; (301) 271-4071.

Mountain Gate. Most people go for the bountiful buffet, which has been drawing motorists off Route 15 and vacationers out of the Catoctin Mountains for a long time. For many devotees, the carving station raises the bar of this buffet over others. Lunch buffet Monday through Friday; evening buffet Monday through Thursday; breakfast buffet Saturday and Sunday. 133 Frederick Rd. (301) 241-5038.

⊨ LODGING

The Cascade Inn, Cascade, Md. This mountain inn is minutes from Thurmont. Once the home of an aide to Robert E. Lee, the Georgian mansion is spacious and graceful, surrounded by gardens and mountain breezes. 14700 Eyler Ave.; (301) 241-4161; www.thecascadeinn.com.

Cozy Inn, Thurmont, Md. If you want a guarantee that you can sleep in a room that some notable political figure once occupied, this is the place. For many years, it's been the rest stop for White House staffers accompanying the president at Camp David. Cabins and rooms are named for presidents and statesmen and decorated in their honor. 103 Frederick Rd.; (301) 271-4301; www.cozyvillage.com.

☕ To Do Along the Way

Have a Picnic at a Covered Bridge:
- **Loy's Station,** south of Thurmont, Md., on Old Frederick Road. Constructed in 1848, the bridge has been rebuilt, but its original timbers are intact over the ninety-foot span over Owens Creek. There are picnic tables in the adjacent park.
- **Roddy Road,** north of Thurmont, Md., and Route 15 on Roddy Road. The forty-foot span over Owens Creek was built in 1858. Picnic tables, the creek, a nice spot.

Pick Your Own Fruit and Berries. Catoctin Mountain Orchard, Route 15, Thurmont. Pace the kids or else it's over way too soon. (301) 271-2737; www.catoctinmountainorchard.com.

See the Animals at Catoctin Wildlife Preserve. A thirty-five acre zoo and park featuring intimate exhibits and educational displays. With a fairly high admission fee, it's not a place to breeze through quickly. But rarely do you get this kind of up close peek at such an array of animals. Open daily, April through October. 13019 Catoctin Furnace Rd.; (301) 271-3180; www.cwpzoo.com.

Visit Cunningham Falls. Less than ten minutes from Thurmont on West 77, these falls have been captivating visitors since the 1930s. An accessible trail and boardwalk lead to the falls; follow signs for falls parking at Cunningham Falls State Park.

⚓ EXPLORING THE COUNTRYSIDE

Catoctin Mountain Park, Thurmont. Visit the historic charcoal pits that fueled Catoctin Furnace and hike to amazing vistas at Blue Ridge Overlook—an easy hike. From Water Street in Thurmont, travel west on Route 77. www.nps.gov/cato.

Cunningham Falls State Park, Thurmont. The lake and hiking trails make nice outdoor day trips, followed by dinner in town. From Water Street in Thurmont, travel west on Route 77. www.dnr.state.md.us/publiclands/western/cunninghamfalls.

Whatever road you take south toward Frederick, you'll want to enter Frederick on Route 355, which becomes Market Street. There is no better way to get a sense of the city than by traveling its main thoroughfare. At this north end of Market is Rose Hill Manor, the former home of Governor Thomas Johnson. During the Civil War, when the property was owned by David Thomas, hundreds of soldiers and a few thousand horses of the Union artillery brigade camped here between battles.

City of Frederick

It takes only a couple of minutes to see why downtown Frederick is a recipient of the Great American Main Street Award. The street has the kind of energy you look for in cities, but with the friendliness and scale of a small town. It's the kind of place that visitors leave pondering how they can move there. You meet residents on the street, and they are effusive about how much they love it.

Downtown in the historic City of Frederick.
Photo: Katie Richardson

And why not? This small city is a lively center for arts, dining, and entertainment. There are shops and galleries featuring fine arts, artisan jewelry, and handmade clothing. For performing arts, within a few dozen steps on Patrick Street, you find the Maryland Ensemble Theater, the Weinberg Center for Performing Arts, and the Frederick Arts Council's Cultural Arts Center, which hosts a number of small theater and dance companies. For dining, the range of cuisine is surprising for a city its size. In a couple of blocks, the cuisine covers the world, including Thai, Mexican, Indian, Spanish, and Ethiopian. And there is nightlife, too. So you can tour the countryside during the day and spend an evening or two in town.

And Frederick is a splendid place for a walk. The commercial downtown is roughly divided into three districts: Market Street, Patrick Street, and East Street. Patrick Street is particularly popular for its bohemian feel and distinctive shops, while East Street is famous for antique dealers. All of Frederick is rich in independently owned businesses and easily accessible on foot.

Historic downtown Frederick is an architectural wonder, exhibiting an expansive range of styles. Its historic district is considered the largest contiguous group of historic structures in Maryland. If you pick up a walking tour brochure from the visitor center at 19 E. Church Street, you can learn about Frederick's history while walking from one building to the next. The list of notable figures who have occupied those buildings is nearly as impressive. Among them are John Hanson, who held the title of chair of the Second Continental Congress as President of the United States Congress Assembled, and Francis Scott Key, the lawyer who wrote the "Star Spangled Banner."

Downtown Frederick has made a real commitment to public art. A series of outdoor murals called "Angels in the Architecture," by local artist William Cochran, adorns a number of buildings and structures. One of the more striking is a huge mural on the Carroll Street Bridge over Carroll Creek (between E. Patrick and E. All Saints streets). Cochran's *trompe l'oeil*, or "trick of the eye," mural transformed a garden-variety concrete bridge into a rustic, ivy-covered stone bridge. Cochran's other murals around town are a source of delight—and sometimes amusement. At the corner of West Church and North Market streets, it's not unusual to see someone look up and ask directions of the bearded figure in the mural ÒEarthbound."

Be sure to stroll down Carroll Creek Promenade. To the delight of walkers and morning joggers, the creek flows through the city with a pathway on either side. In summer, if you stroll the creek to quiet Baker Park, a forty-four acre downtown gem, you might hear an outdoor concert or see children's theater.

📖 FREDERICK WALKING TOURS

Frederick is a city of stunning architecture, from churches to mansions. Stop in the Frederick Visitor Center, 19 E. Church St., for a self-guided walking tour brochure or to begin a seasonal weekend guided walking tour.

🏛 HISTORICAL SITES AND HERITAGE MUSEUMS IN AND AROUND FREDERICK

Beatty-Cramer House

The original part of the house, built circa 1732, is the oldest structure in Frederick County and has been called one of the most important historical resources in Maryland. The main house consists of the original structure and the "new" addition, built in 1855 by the Cramer family. There also is a two-story springhouse beside Israel Creek and smokehouse. The house had become so dilapidated that in 1985 the owners offered it up to the local fire department for training, first allowing the Frederick County Landmark Foundation to document its history. During their research they recognized the value of the property. Blake

Gambrill Mill Visitor Center, down the Worthington Farm trail.
Photo: Steven L. Spring

Construction Company, owner of the land, sold the buildings and land to the Foundation for five bucks. Open by appointment. 9010 Liberty Rd., Route 26; (301) 668-2086); www.frederickcountylandmarksfoundation.org.

Historical Society of Frederick County

This museum, in an 1829 mansion, is the best place to begin your Frederick touring. More than a house museum, the historical society uses the house as a backdrop to tell the story of Frederick and the region. The collection of fine and decorative arts, as well as the collection of tall clocks, is extensive. The society sponsors walking tours and other educational programs. The museum library is open to the public. Monday through Saturday, 10 to 4; 24 E. Church St., Frederick; (301) 663-1188; www.hsfcinfo.org.

Monocacy National Battlefield

This battle marks the final attempt by the Confederate Army to invade the North. General Jubal Early was

Monocacy National Battlefield, where the Confederate Army made its final attempt to invade the North. Photo: Steven L. Spring

marching eighteen thousand men toward Washington, DC, July 9, 1864. It was part of Robert E. Lee's strategy to take the pressure off the South by drawing Union forces into the defense of the Union capital. Greatly outnumbered, Union General Lew Wallace's men held out for an entire day of battle before being forced to flee for their lives. But they had delayed Early's march to Washington long enough. By the time he reached the outskirts of the capital, the Union was waiting and repulsed the attack. Had Early been able to keep to his plan, the focus and momentum of the war might have shifted. Hence, the Battle of Monocacy is known as the "Battle That Saved Washington."

You can take an auto tour of the battlefield, but two of the best attractions are on foot. The Worthington Farm trail down to the ford on the Monocacy gives a soldier's view of climbing out of the creek to ascend Brooks Hill. Near the visitor center, the accessible boardwalk trail provides an up-close view of the battle action over the road and rail bridges. Gambrill Mill Visitor Center open daily. www.nps.org/mono.

National Museum of Civil War Medicine

Traveling the Piedmont you can't help but notice the number of homes and churches displaying signs marking the site of a Civil War hospital. You get the impression that the entire countryside was engaged in the care of the sick, dying, and dead. You would be right. Just as war tends to bring about technological innovations, the Civil War had a profound impact on the development of medicine and how we care for the dead. This museum takes you there, and it works at various levels for people of all ages. It also changes the way you think about field medicine in the Civil War, which we're often led to believe was "amputate first, ask questions later." Yes, the backdrop is the Civil War, but this really is a story about the practice of medicine—just another example of how America happened along The Journey Through Hallowed Ground.

Monday through Saturday, 10 to 5; Sunday, 11 to 5. 48 E. Patrick St.; www.civilwarmed.org.

Roger Brooke Taney House

The site interprets the life of the fifth Chief Justice of the United States, as well as the times in which he lived. Taney administered the oath of office to five U.S. presidents and was the author of several important decisions. For many Americans, he is remembered only as the author of the Dred-Scott decision, which, among other things, declared that African Americans had no right to U.S. citizenship. The home is operated by The Historical Society of Frederick County. Open Saturday and Sunday, April through December. 121 S. Bentz St.; (301) 663-7880; www.hsfcinfo.org.

Rose Hill Manor Park & Children's Museum

Rose Hill Manor was the home of Maryland's first elected governor, Thomas Johnson, the man credited with naming the nation's capital for George Washington. There is something for everyone here. The farm museum presents late nineteenth-century and early twentieth-century agricultural practices and farm family life. You see a farm kitchen, carpentry shop, butcher shop, and a steam-powered tractor. The exhibit of agricultural hand tools and machinery is a hit with young men in particular. The tour of the main house is led by costumed interpreters. Open Monday through Saturday, 10 to 4, April through October; weekends in November. 1611 N. Market; (301) 694-1650; www.rosehillmuseum.com.

Schifferstadt Architectural Museum

Sure, this is *the* place for Oktoberfest—as the annual poster says: beer, food, entertainment! But this stone house is also the oldest building in Frederick City and an example of how a group of people can get together to save a bit of history. Built in 1756 by Elias Bruner, whose family settled in Frederick in 1730, it has been called one of the best examples of early German colonial architecture. The museum interprets more than architecture; it recounts the migration of German immigrants who came south from the Gettysburg area in search of affordable farmland—after having located there from Philadelphia for the same reason. Today, German is still the most common ancestry in Maryland. In 1974, plans to demolish the building for a new gas station rallied the Frederick County Landmarks Foundation to purchase the house, which has since been studied and restored. 1110 Rosemont Ave., Exit 14 off Route 15; Wednesday through Sunday, 10 to 4, April through October, and by appointment. (301) 668-6088; www.frederickcountylandmarksfoundation.org.

♨ EATING OUT, HANGING OUT

In Frederick

Acacia Fusion Bistro. East meets west with flare. You can make an evening from the appetizer menu with the likes of ginger-soy glazed chicken skewers, vegetable spring rolls served with a cucumber salad, and grilled cognac-marinated lamb chops—just for starters. Open daily; handicapped accessible. 129 N. Market St.; (301) 694-3015.

Beans and Bagels. The name doesn't quite say it all. There are pastries, sandwiches and soups, and other snacks. Bring the newspaper. 49 E. Patrick St.

Brewer's Alley Restaurant and Brewery. Brewers Alley was the name of Frederick's nineteenth-century brewer's district. Brewer's Alley today is a brew pub located in the historic town hall building, brewing up an assortment of staples and seasonal ales. Outdoor seating in summer; music at night. A fine reason to secure a room within walking distance. 124 N. Market St.; (301) 631-0089; www.brewers_alley.com.

Firestones Restaurant and Bar. Local bands and open mike nights are the nighttime attractions. Open for lunch and dinner, with brunch on Sundays. The second floor seating overlooks the street and long bar downstairs—classic Frederick. 105 N. Market St; (301) 663-0330; www.firestonesrestaurant.com.

Market Street Café. It's a bookstore, coffee shop, sandwich place, ice cream scoop shop. Nice place to hang out. 14 N. Market St. (301) 695–0222.

Proof Artisan Bakery. Advertised as a bakery specializing in breads and sweet treats, but its sandwiches and salads draw crowds too. It's a casual, order-at-the-counter place. Don't bother boxing up that big chocolate cupcake thing "to eat later"; you're lucky if you make it to the corner without devouring it. Open Monday through Saturday, 6 a.m. to 8 p.m.; 12 E. Patrick. (301) 668–2303.

Tajitu. Traditional Ethiopian cuisine served in the old Snow White Hamburger Grill. Choose from traditional Ethiopian seating or upright Americana. Either way, make room for appetizers like Senge Karya (peppers stuffed with sautéed fresh tomatoes, onions, garlic, and shallots served with Injera), Yemisir Sambusa (pastry stuffed with spiced lentils, onions, and green peppers), and other zesty and spicy offerings. Lots for vegetarians to choose too. 9 E. Patrick St.; (301) 631-6800.

The Tasting Room. Pleasing take on regional dishes, such as oak-planked rockfish, mix it up with the likes of porcini risotto and Cuban pork. Huge storefront dining room windows offer a view of historic downtown Frederick. Closed Sundays. 101 N. Market St.; (240) 379-7772.

Vignola Market. Mozzarella is made fresh daily in this authentic Italian deli, where the offerings include a menu of sandwiches on crusty rolls. The fare also includes freshly made pastas, sauces, sausages, cheeses, and breads. Closed Sundays. 9 East Church St.; (301) 620-0077.

Westside Café. Bagels in the morning, wraps and salads for lunch, and dinner entrees in the evening. Beer and wine served in the casual dining room, where live acoustic music fills the air in the evening. Open daily. 1A W. 2nd St.; (301) 418-6886. For music schedule, check www.westside-café.com.

Zest. Since its first incarnation in Montgomery County, Zest has been dedicated to using local ingredients whenever available. It has a loyal following who now make the trip to Frederick. Creative seafood, Maryland rabbit, and savory meat renditions are the focus; not for vegetarians. 200 S. Market St.; (301) 620-7480; www.eatatzest.com.

Near Frederick

Barbara Fritchie Candy Stick Restaurant, Frederick. Not to be confused with the museum also named for Fritchie, this place does not go back quite to the Civil War, but it dates to 1910 (since 1960 at this location). Real food, great pies in a diner atmosphere. Breakfast served all day! Look for the giant candy cane. 1513 W. Patrick St. (Route 40); (301) 662-2500.

Eunice's Restaurant, north of Frederick. Great fried chicken, truly homemade food, and friendly people, right on the Journey's mainline. Route 15 and Biggs Ford Rd., Frederick; (301) 898-3490.

✠ Distinctive Shops and Stops

Amber Coast. Featuring handcrafted works from craftsmen in "New Europe," such as glassworks from Poland and the Czech Republic, Baltic jewelry, and tapestries from Latvia. 113 E. Patrick St.; (301) 631-2217.

Accentuates. A tiny shop that defies description, selling artful renditions of everyday items such as switch plates, hooks and doorbells—again, it defies description. Open daily; 116 A E. Patrick St.; (301) 695-5787.

Dancing Bear Toys and Gifts. Big kids and little ones will find inventive toys and games, music, and children's books by Maryland authors and illustrators. Closed Sunday; handicapped accessible.12 N. Market St.; (301) 631-9300.

Delaplaine Visual Arts Education Center. Housed in the historic Mountain City Mill building, the education center features gallery exhibits, an emerging artists gallery, and special programs. The gallery store features ceramics, paintings, prints, jewelry, and woodworking by local artists. Open Monday through Saturday, 9:30 to 5:30. 40 S. Carroll St.; (301) 698-0656; www.delaplaine.org.

Everedy Square/Shab Row. A Frederick landmark, three blocks of historic buildings housing antique dealers, a farmers market, and specialty shops. 4 through 136 N. East St.

Le Savon. Handcrafted soaps, lotions, and skin care made right there in the shop. Guys, you can go too; they even have a soap called Dude—you use soap, right? 10 E. Church St.; (301) 694-5002; www.lesavon.com.

Maryland Ensemble Theatre. The only full-time professional company along The Journey Through Hallowed Ground produces contemporary plays in a downtown venue. See the website for what's on the boards. 31 W. Patrick St.; (301) 694-4744; www.marylandensemble.org.

McGuire Fine Art. The Disney art tends to get top billing here, but there's an extensive offering of jewelry, ceramics, and sculpture. 110 N. Market St.; (301) 695-6567.

The Muse. A popular stop for out-of-towners and locals alike, selling creative handmade gifts, pottery, crafts, and art. 19 N. Market St. (301) 666-3632

Trail House. A terrific locally owned outdoor gear and apparel store—a rare find. 17 S. Market St.; (301) 694-8448.

⊨ LODGING

In Frederick

Hill House Bed & Breakfast. An elegant 1870 Victorian townhouse with four guest rooms, each decorated with original artwork and period furnishings. Restaurants and downtown entertainment are just out the door. 12 W. Third St.; (301) 682-4111; www.itlink.com/hillhouse.

Hollerstown Hill. On a quiet street in downtown Frederick, this Victorian has four guest rooms, all with claw-foot tubs, one with its own private porch. Walking distance to shops and restaurants; special features include a billiards room and wireless Internet. 4 Clarke Pl.; (301) 228-3630; www.hollerstownhill.com.

Catoctin Inn, Buckeystown, Md. The historic manor house, circa 1780, is known equally well for its dining as for its twenty elegant guest rooms. On weekends, there is music in the dining room. Think truffles and harp music. 3919 Buckeystown Pike; (301) 874-5555; www.catoctinn.com.

Inn at Buckeystown, Buckeystown, Md. The 1897 Victorian mansion in the heart of the historic village provides luxury accommodations in a quiet setting. The inn's afternoon tea has a dedicated following and is an especially fine way to pass a rainy afternoon—it's those little cucumber sandwiches that do it. Several times a year the inn hosts murder-mystery theater and other themed theatrical presentations. 3521 Buckeystown Pike; (301) 874-5755; www.innatbuckeystown.com.

To Do Along the Way

Take a **Candlelight Ghost Tour** of Frederick. Tours meet in front of Brewer's Alley. (301) 668-8922; www.marylandghosttours.com.

Carrollton House built in 1724 by Charles Carroll, a signer of the Declaration of Independence. Photo: Steven L. Spring

Take a Horse-drawn Carriage Ride through Frederick. Group tours and intimate rides for two (or one) available. Frederick Tour and Carriage Company. (301) 845-7001; ww.frederickcarriage.com.

Take a Scenic Railroad Ride. The Walkersville Southern Railroad leaves from the old depot, just across from the railroad museum in Walkersville, about five minutes north of Frederick. There are mystery dinner theater excursions and the very popular fall foliage trains. You can even rent the caboose for private parties. Arrive early to spend time in the museum. Call or see website for directions. (877) 363-9777; www.wsrr.org.

 EXPLORING THE COUNTRYSIDE

Historic Sites near Frederick

Antietam National Battlefield, Sharpsburg, Md. September 17, 1862, is known as the bloodiest day in American history. More soldiers died at the Battle of Antietam than American soldiers in the Revolutionary War, War of 1812, Mexican War, and Spanish-American War combined. Corn was a cause. After the Confederate victory in Second Manassas (Bull Run), General Robert E. Lee decided to take the war into the North. There were many strategic reasons, but there also was a need to feed his troops. By drawing Union attention to the North in September, Virginia farmers could harvest without being harassed by Federal troops. And Southern troops could avail themselves of the bounty north of the Potomac River.

The best way to tour Antietam is on bicycle—especially the part west of Sharpsburg. Everyone should experience a late afternoon atop the battlefield observation tower. The town of Sharpsburg has a decidedly low-key attitude toward the battlefield. There's an artifacts' shop and a Civil War art gallery. Nutters on Potomac Street is the place for ice cream. The town also observes the battle with an annual street festival. Open daily; www.nps.gov/anti.

Dahlgren Chapel, Boonsboro, Md. The chapel was built in 1881 by Sarah Madeleine Vinton Dahlgren, whose summer home is now South Mountain Inn. The chapel primarily served as her family's private church while away from their home in Washington, DC. Madeleine Dahlgren is best known for her book *South Mountain Magic*, which recounts folklore and ghost stories she gathered from locals, and as the wife of Rear Admiral Dahlgren, U.S.N.—inventor of the Dahlgren Gun. The chapel was purchased and restored by the Central Maryland Heritage League. Currently, indoor access is very limited, but the chapel's site in Turner's Gap makes even outdoor access worth the trip. Route 40 Alternate; www.cmhl.org.

Monocacy Aqueduct on the C&O Canal, Dickerson, Md. It has been called the finest canal feature in America, and after more than thirty years of being held together with metal bands and pins, it has been restored to its glory. In order to carry the 184-mile canal over wide creeks and rivers, eleven aqueducts were constructed. This one, over the Monocacy River, is constructed of huge granite blocks with seven arches in its 438-foot span. It truly is a thing of beauty. Just a short walk from the trailhead parking lot, there is a barrier-free trail leading to the span. There are interpretive markers and historical photographs at the site recounting the canal days and the efforts of citizens to restore the aqueduct. Bring a picnic lunch and take a walk along the C&O. Open daily. www.nps.gov/choh.

South Mountain State Battlefield, atop South Mountain, Frederick County, Md. In recent years this battle has begun to receive attention from scholars and activists for its significance. It was fought along several miles of ridgeline, with action seen in the towns of Burkittsville and Middletown, both of which became the sites of impromptu hospitals. Most of the battlefields are now forested, but there are monuments at the three gaps along the front. Gathland, at the southern end of the battle line, is a state park preserving the summer estate of Civil War journalist George Alfred Townsend. The Appalachian Trail traverses the ridge here, which makes it possible to hike from Gathland to Washington Monument at the north end. For information and narrative, see Central Maryland Heritage League's website, www.cmhl.org/bsm.html.

Washington Monument State Park, Middletown, Md. The main attraction of this 108-acre park is the first monument ever built to the first U.S. President, a milk-jug shaped stone monument built in 1827. The views from the top of the monument are wondrous, as Civil War scouts from both armies could attest. The monument, by virtue of its shape, is certainly whimsical. According to the tale, most of Boonsboro's five hundred residents paraded up South Mountain in the early morning of July 4 to build the monument. They used a dry-stack technique to build a fifty-four-foot base and a tower of fifteen feet in one day, then returned in autumn to complete the tower to a height of thirty feet. Twice the monument has been reduced to rubble by weather and wear. The current structure was rebuilt by the Civilian Conservation Corp in 1936 to a height of thirty-four feet. You can drive the 1.5 miles from Route 40-A, but a nice walk along the Appalachian Trail is highly recommended. Route 40 Alternate, in Turner's Gap. Open daily till 5 p.m. www.dnr.state.md.us/publiclands/western/Washington.

Wineries, Farms and Special Stops

Berrywine Plantation/Linganore Winecellars, Mt. Airy, Md. The specialty here is old world fruit wines. The Medieval Mead recalls wines crafted long ago—the crowd at the annual Maryland Renaissance loves it. www.linganorewines.com.

Catoctin Mountain Orchard. Home grown berries, vegetables, and fruit, along with a vast assortment of jams, sauces, and preserves. Kids love to "pick your own." 15036 N. Franklinville Rd. (at the junction with Route 15); www.catoctinmountainorchard.com.

Catoctin Pottery. Potter Susan Hansen's studio is a slight detour off Route 15. Her studio is in Lewis Mill, built in the early nineteenth century (see her website for a photo of the mill). Hansen's studio is welcoming to browsers and travelers; her style ranges from traditional Appalachian folk pottery to whimsical renditions of Southwestern desert flora. Open Monday through Saturday, 10 a.m. to 5 p.m. 3205 Poffenberger Rd., Jefferson, Md.; (301) 371-4274; www.catoctinpottery.com.

Elk Run Vineyards, Mt. Airy, Md. Located along scenic Route 26 east of Frederick, Elk Run is Maryland's only vineyard producing a Pinot Noir. Dinner events at the winery are popular among locals and travelers alike. 15113 Liberty Rd.; (410) 775-2513; www.elkrun.com.

Loew Vinyards, Mount Airy, Md. One of the longest established Maryland vineyards offering a small selection of craft blends. Liberty Rd.; (301) 831-5464; www.loewvinyards.net.

Outdoor Recreation

Frederick Municipal Forest, north of Frederick, west of Route 15. Remote unpaved roads in a seven-thousand-acre forest, wedged between Cunningham Falls and Gambrill state parks. Offering the most scenic bicycling in the region. www.dnr.state.md.us/publiclands/western/fcw.html.

Gambrill State Park, northwest of Frederick. The legacy of James Gambrill, a Frederick conservation advocate, the park was purchased by Frederick residents for use as a city park. It is now a state park with hiking trails, a scenic drive, and three overlooks. www.dnr.state.md.us/publiclands/western/gambrill.html.

Small Towns

Brunswick, Md. Off Route 340, about nine miles west of the intersection with Route 15, Brunswick is a C&O Canal town with a fine railroad museum, antique shops, and a café in a church that is itself a reason to visit. See Potomac Legacy Loop scenic drive.

Brunswick, Maryland – full of antique shops. Photo: Steven L. Spring

New Market, Md. Eight miles east of Frederick on Route 144 and bypassed by motorists on busy I-70 south of town, New Market hums with antique browsers each weekend. There are too many dealers to even begin listing, and, according to browsers, the proximity of so many dealers creates bargain environment. A few non-antique stores bear mentioning. New Market General Store, while primarily a gift shop, carries a broad assortment of candies and nuts—three kinds of black licorice! Blues Barbecue is in the back of the store. At Mallard's Café (known until recently as the Village Tea Shop), save room for the fruit pies, especially the mixed berry with lemon crust. In a state of pie euphoria, stumble over to the Little Pottery Shop, where the local and regional artisans are featured.

Drive southwest from Frederick on Route 15 (also here, Route 340) for several miles. Then Route 15 breaks south toward the Point of Rocks and the river. You also can take scenic Route 351, Ballenger Creek Road, south all the way to Point of Rocks. En route, you will pass **Cooling Springs Farm**, a secret station on the Underground Railroad that is open to tours by appointment (see www.coolingspring.org). A mile further down the road is the intersection with Point of Rocks Road, which leads right to Route 15 and another eight miles to Brunswick (see Potomac Legacy Loop).

Point of Rocks

Point of Rocks is the last stop in Maryland along the Journey. For such a tiny settlement, it got plenty of attention during the Civil War, when Confederate snipers made a habit of harassing railroad and canal operations. While passing through the settlement, there are a few stops that help put the place and its location into historical view.

🏛 HISTORICAL SITES

C&O Canal and Civil War Trail

Take a few minutes to head to the river, following the boat access road. Interpretive markers describe the skirmishes and sharpshooting that took place during the war in efforts to control the canal and railroad.

Point of Rocks Bridge

The bridge was the focus of Union concerns in their efforts to guard against sabotage of the railroad and canal. Rebel snipers fired from the Virginia side at Union pickets. In July 1864, Colonel John Mosby and his Rangers attacked the Union garrison in support of General Jubal Early's attempted invasion of the capital. The skirmish lasted less than an hour, with the Confederates retreating following the arrival of Union cavalry. To see the eponymous rocks, cross the bridge into Virginia and visit the boat launch on the shoreline.

The railroad station at Point of Rocks, constructed in 1875.
Photo: Steven L. Spring

Point of Rocks Railroad Station

Sleepy Point of Rocks, a remote outpost in 1830, received national attention as a "point of contention" between the railroad and canal companies. Each claimed the narrow right-of-way between the river and the cliff, a battle which stalled both projects for four years. Perhaps the significance of the location in part explains the extravagant design bestowed upon this minor rural depot when constructed in 1875. It also demonstrates the primacy of railroads in the decades following the Civil War. As an example of Victorian Gothic Revival public architecture, it ranks among the best and least known examples. Today, the station is a commuter stop on the MARC line to Washington, D.C. Although the interior of the building is not open to the public, the exterior is well worth up-close appreciation.

St. Paul's Church

Opened for worship in 1843, St. Paul's illustrates an irony of Antebellum America. The building was constructed using enslaved laborers under contract with a local plantation, with money donated primarily by families who assisted fugitive slaves in their escape north. Soon after the church's opening, according to accounts, it became a station on the Underground Railroad—one of the first such stops north of the Potomac in this valley. Timbers were cut from trees on church property, and bricks were made from the soil here. The building was appropriated by Union troops during the Civil War; they used it as a hospital, mess hall, and headquarters. The damage exacted on the building was compensated by Congress following the war. The church was abandoned in the 1880s when the congregation moved to a newer chapel in town. It was restored in the 1960s when the congregants sold the chapel to a Baptist congregation. Ballenger Creek Pike, Point of Rocks, Md.

The Soldiers' National Cemetery at Gettysburg National Military Park.
Photo: Katie Lawhon

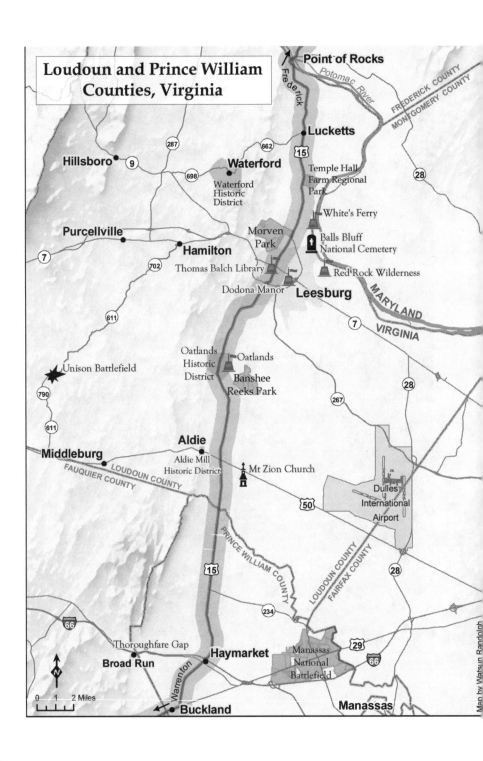

Loudoun and Prince William Counties, Virginia

Point of Rocks

Frederick

Potomac River

FREDERICK COUNTY
MONTGOMERY COUNTY

Luckets

287

662

15

28

Hillsboro

9

Waterford

698

Waterford
Historic
District

Temple Hall
Farm Regional
Park

White's Ferry

Purcellville

Morven
Park

Balls Bluff
National Cemetery

7

Hamilton

702

Thomas Balch Library

Red Rock Wilderness

Dodona Manor

Leesburg

MARYLAND

VIRGINIA

7

611

Oatlands
Historic
District

Oatlands

28

Unison Battlefield

Banshee
Reeks Park

790

267

611

Aldie

Aldie Mill
Historic District

Mt Zion Church

Middleburg

FAUQUIER COUNTY

LOUDOUN COUNTY

50

Dulles
International
Airport

PRINCE WILLIAM COUNTY

LOUDOUN COUNTY

FAIRFAX COUNTY

28

15

234

66

Thoroughfare Gap

Broad Run

Haymarket

Manassas
National
Battlefield

29

66

Warrenton

N

0   1   2 Miles

Buckland

Manassas

Map by Watson Randolph

— Chapter 2 —

The Journey Through

Loudoun and Prince
William Counties, Virginia

Distance:	37 miles

HIGHLIGHTS ALONG THE JOURNEY THROUGH HALLOWED GROUND.

Miles	Site
0	POTOMAC CROSSING/POINT OF ROCKS BRIDGE
4.0	LUCKETTS
10	WHITE'S FERRY
10.5	BALLS BLUFF NATIONAL CEMETERY
11	HISTORIC LEESBURG: DODONA MANOR, MORVEN PARK, THOMAS BALCH LIBRARY
17	OATLANDS HISTORIC DISTRICT
17.5	BANSHEE REEKS
19	OAK HILL, HOME OF PRESIDENT JAMES MONROE
23	ALDIE MILL HISTORIC DISTRICT AND MOUNT ZION CHURCH.
37	BUCKLAND

Crossing the Potomac River into Loudoun County from Point of Rocks evokes the feeling of turning onto a country road. Gravel driveways extend to the thoroughfare and old houses dot the

Photo: CMW

roadside. As the road opens, Sugarloaf Mountain is seen to the east in Maryland; to the west are the Catoctin Mountains.

The road through Loudoun roughly approximates that of the Old Carolina Road, a storied pathway used by Susquehannock and Iroquois Indians for trade and warfare, and later by European settlers as a migration and trade route. During the Revolutionary War, soldiers marched north, and British prisoners were directed south under forced march. This also is the northern reach of Mosby Heritage Area, recognizing the region reigned by (or harassed by, depending on your allegiances) John Singleton Mosby, whose Rangers employed guerrilla tactics during the Civil War to strike fear into Union soldiers and officers. By Mosby's count, he kept thirty thousand Union soldiers out of the war by distracting them in a six-county area.

Along Route 15 through Loudoun, except for the area around the county seat of Leesburg, the countryside is sparsely settled. Leesburg was a town on the western frontier when it was chartered in 1758, after more than thirty years of settlement of the surrounding area by English, German, Scots-Irish, and African-born and Creole slaves. Like many settlements in the interior,

Leesburg grew up at the junction of two roads. Here the north-south Carolina Road (Route 15) intersected with the Alexandria Road (Route 50), which by the 1750s stretched from the port city west to the Shenandoah Valley.

Modern Leesburg is a delightful courthouse town with a movie theater, restaurants, and galleries. Within the town limits, several new residential and commercial developments have captured the essence of the place, so that even the new seems to fit. Not surprisingly, this old town is home to antique shops and galleries specializing in landscape paintings, but there is a cosmopolitan side, too, found in its trendy restaurants and boutiques.

South of Leesburg, at Oatlands Historic District, the Piedmont vista stretches into the distance. Further on, the view widens on both sides as you travel the subtle high point above two beautiful creeks, Little River and Howsers Run. Just beyond is Oak Hill, home of President James Monroe, where he is said to have penned the Monroe Doctrine. It is for Monroe that this stretch of Route 15 is named.

During the Civil War, all battles in Loudoun were not between the Union and Confederacy. Parts of the Loudoun County remained openly pro-Union, a continual source of conflict, even bloodshed,

TRAVEL ASSISTANCE

Leesburg Visitor Center
Located in the town hall building, the center is open every day. It is staffed on weekends only, but the brochure racks are accessible every day. 25 W. Market Street; (703) 777-2420; www.leesburgva.com/visitors.

Loudoun Convention & Visitor Association
222 Catoctin Circle; (800) 884-9106; www.VisitLoudoun.org.

between friends and family. Bordering the Potomac River, Loudoun saw nearly continuous troop encampments and movements throughout the war, much of it along the Old Carolina Road. Driving south from Leesburg in the early morning hours, you can almost imagine a line of soldiers, horses, and caissons stretching from the Potomac to Aldie in southern Loudoun.

From the River to Leesburg

*O*ne of the great pleasures of traveling The Journey Through Hallowed Ground is driving stretches of open countryside like this one and happening upon its varied roadside attractions. The first of these is reached immediately after you cross the bridge from Point of Rocks.

Patowmack Farm and **Dinner in the Garden**. Right after crossing the Potomac River into Virginia, take the first right onto Route 672. A mile down the road is one of the most distinctive restaurants of the Piedmont. Sitting high atop a bluff overlooking the Potomac and Point of Rocks, Patowmack Farm serves patrons in a greenhouse-like dining room. Most of the food is harvested from the organic operation on site; much of what isn't grown or raised here comes from other nearby farms. The tasting menus have won legions of fans—five- or seven-course selections of appetizer-sized portions. Any fellow looking for the perfect ambiance to pop the question could not go wrong. For lunch, visit the country store for breads, produce, salsas and other picnic items. 42461 Lovettsville Road, Lovettsville; (540) 822-9017; www.patowmackfarm.com.

———

A mile from the Point of Rocks Bridge is **My Wits End Antiques**. Several rooms of collectables and antique tools, toys, and furnishings—everything from elegant tea sets to rustic mauls, mallets and planers, all lorded over by the neighbors' cat, who walks down the hill each morning to hang out. 12810 James Monroe Hwy.; (703) 777-1561; www.witsaboutus.com.

Lucketts

Another few miles down the road comes the historic settlement of Lucketts, Va. This country crossroads attracts antique- and collectable-hunters and bluegrass lovers, sometimes at the same time. The Old Lucketts School, a handsome century-old building, is now a community center and the center of the community. The annual Lucketts Fair is the genuine article, featuring a pie contest, crafts, contests for the best tomato and zucchini, and lots of food. Even the bees pitch in with a honey-making demonstration. The fair is usually held on the fourth weekend in August. www.luckettsfair.com.

Bluegrass at Lucketts is a casual series at the Old Lucketts School. The Sunday evening concerts host regional bluegrass favorites, as well as a few internationally known artists. The late, great Bob Paisley performed there with his band the Southern Grass, a tradition carried on today with son Dan as the front man. www.lucketts.org.

The village's other attractions are all on one corner, at the intersection with Stumptown Road.

Beekeepers Cottage. Cottage is the operative word, as in cottage style. The store deals in furnishings, linens, slipcovers, home accessories, and bath and body products. Open daily, 10 to 5. (703) 771-9006; www.beekeeperscottage.com.

Old Lucketts Store. You could say that the Lucketts Store is located in the former post office and general store, but it would be more accurate to say the store is located in, around, and on top of the old structure. Built in 1910, the home was the Lucketts family home. It's an over-flowing assortment of indoor and outdoor furnishings, vintage linens and clothes, tools, whatnots, prints . . . you get it. Open daily, 10 to 5. (703) 779-0268; www.luckettstore.com.

Really Great Finds. Garden iron, outdoor planters, prints, clocks, phones, you name it. Open weekends. www.reallygreatfinds.com.

Sailing south from Lucketts toward Leesburg under Catoctin skies, there are two recent entries to the Virginia world of wineries: **Hidden Brook** (www.hiddenbrookwinery.com) and **Lost Creek** (www.lostcreekwinery.com). Follow the signs.

South of the Point of Rocks Bridge and just north of Leesburg, the left turn onto Limestone School Road leads to **Temple Hall Farm**, a Northern Virginia Regional Park. It's a 286-acre working farm that raises goats, hogs, peacocks, chickens, ducks, and sheep. The farm offers tours to students during the week; it's open to the public for tours on weekends in season. Loudoun kids know it as the autumn home of the Corn MAiZE. www.nvrpa.org/templehall.

A mile north of Leesburg is the turn-off to **White's Ferry**, the last working ferry on the Potomac. Pick up a picnic lunch in Leesburg and take a short trip down to the river. It's a quick ride to the Maryland shore, one kids will talk about for a long time. There are picnic tables at the C&O Canal National Park. From Route 15

White's Ferry.
Photo: Courtesy of Loudoun Convention and Visitors Association

King Street, Leesburg, Virginia. Photo: CMW

north of Leesburg, follow Edwards Ferry Road east toward the ferry. It operates daily, 5 a.m. to 11 p.m.

Just before the Route 15 Bypass heads east, there is a right turn on Tutt Lane to a Civil War Trails marker overlooking the fields of **Morven Park**.

Leesburg

Leesburg is an historic town that celebrates its past but doesn't live there. Within historic buildings you can find exceptional, contemporary food and cafes, visit a spa for a massage or facial, and shop for trendy clothing. True to expectations of such an historic settlement, Leesburg has antiques shops—enough to satisfy a range of interests, from historic prints and maps, to furnishings and home décor, to antiquarian books.

More than any town along The Journey Through Hallowed Ground, Leesburg has significant sites linked to significant people and events of the twentieth century. Charles Houston argued important Civil Rights cases at the courthouse. The home of Virginia Governor Westmoreland Davis is a magnificent twentieth-century mansion and estate known as Morven Park. And there is Dodona Manor, the home of General George C. Marshall. Here the general hosted presidents and diplomats and crafted the plan to create peace and prosperity in post-World War II Europe. He also took time to engage in civic life by participating in local causes and community organizations.

Another mid-twentieth century gem is the Tallyho movie theater on Market Street, inducement enough to spend an evening in Leesburg.

📖 TOURS

African American Heritage Tour of Leesburg. A self-guided walking tour; pick up a copy at the Loudoun Museum, 16 Loudoun Street SW, (703) 777-7427; or at the Balch Library; 208 W. Market St.; (703) 737-7195; www.leesburgva.gov/services/library.

Exploring Leesburg: A Guide to History and Architecture. This 158-page self-guided walking tour documents 160 buildings and sites within the historic town limits. Available at the Loudoun Museum, 16 W. Loudoun; the Leesburg Bookstore, 13 Wirt St. SW (around the corner from the Museum); and Leesburg Town Hall, 25 W. Market St.

Leesburg Guided Walking Tours, offered by the Loudoun Museum. These two-hour tours use the historic buildings and homes of Leesburg to bring to life the town's 250-year history. Private tours are also available. Call (703) 777-7427, or consult the museum website, www.loudounmuseum.org.

Leesburg Historic District.
Photo: Courtesy of Loudoun Convention and Visitors Association

Balls Bluff National Cemetery, tombs of unknown Civil War soldiers.
Photo: CMW

Loudoun County's African American Communities: A Tour Map and Guide. The guide provides an overview of African American heritage in the county through its churches and communities. Available at the Balch Library, 208 W. Market St.

🏛 HISTORICAL SITES AND HERITAGE MUSEUMS

Ball's Bluff National Cemetery

This half-acre cemetery and National Historic Landmark lies within Ball's Bluff Battlefield Regional Park, about two miles from downtown Leesburg. Inside the perimeter of its stone walls lie the remains of fifty-four Civil War soldiers, fifty-three of whom are "unknowns." Surrounding the cemetery is the lovely Ball's Bluff Park, a wooded oasis for the adjacent suburban communities. The view of the Potomac and the Maryland riverside from the bluffs is among the finest in the Piedmont. An interpretive trail tells the story of this peculiar battle that began because a Union reconnaissance party mistook trees in the moonlight for a Confederate encampment. A series of errors and miscalculations resulted in 1,720 Union soldiers standing in an open field while backed up to the steep palisades. More than half were wounded, captured, killed, or missing. To visit, follow signs on Battlefield Parkway East. (703) 352-5900; www.nvrpa.org/ballsbluffbattle.

Dodona Manor

Built in the first half of the nineteenth century, the estate was the home of General George C. Marshall from 1941 until his death in 1959. Marshall is arguably one of the most influential Americans of the twentieth century. While most Americans are familiar with the term the "Marshall Plan," the decades have diminished public appreciation of the essential role of the plan in rebuilding European society after World War II, leading to the affluent, stable democracies of Europe. Marshall was awarded the Nobel Peace Prize, the only military officer ever so honored.

The home, which opened to visitors for the first time in 2005, reveals a man who was at ease with small-town life, who participated in community groups and garden clubs when at home. The kitchen and family room, which depict home gadgets of a simpler era, show as much about the Marshalls' down-to-earth values as they do of the era. Marshall's home is sure to become one of the region's most-visited historic sites. Currently open weekends only; check website for updates. 217 Edwards Ferry Road. (703) 777-1880; www.georgecmarshall.org.

Loudoun Courthouse

Although the current building is a relative newcomer, built in 1895, the site dates from the town's founding in 1758, when Nicholas Minor set aside two half-acre lots for the courthouse and jail. Two previous courthouses stood at this location. Gone are the public privies, the market, stocks, and whipping post; but the history—demonstrating both the best and least of American heritage—remains. The former site of slave auctions, it also is the site of memorable arguments by civil rights lawyer Charles Houston, effectively challenging the notion of separate-but-equal. In 1825, President John Quincy Adams and former President Monroe escorted General Lafayette to the courthouse during his final tour of the U.S.—an event that drew ten thousand people to Leesburg. 10 North King Street.

Loudoun Museum

Permanent and rotating exhibits interpret the county's history and offer a local perspective on national events— for example, a recent exhibit on the French and Indian War in Loudoun. A restored eighteenth-century log cabin houses the museum's shop. The museum hosts a full schedule of educational programs throughout the year. For kids, the 1820's children's Discovery Room is a favorite. Monday and Wednesday through Saturday, 10 to 5; Sundays, 1-5; Tuesdays, by appointment. 16 Loudoun St., SW; (703) 777-7427; www.loudounmuseum.org.

Morven Park.
Photo: Courtesy of Loudoun Convention and Visitors Association

Morven Park

The home of former Virginia Governor Westmoreland Davis, the only Loudouner elected to the state's highest office. It was built in the early 1800s by the family of Thomas Swann, Jr., also a governor—of Maryland. Extensive restorations are planned for the Governor's Mansion 2006-2008, but the estate's other popular attractions remain open during that time. The Winmill Carriage Collection contains an extraordinary exhibit of conveyances built from the middle 1800s through the early twentieth century. The Hansom Cab, Norwegian Cariole, and the Million & Guilet Caleche are just a few of the coaches on display. The Museum of Hounds and Hunting displays foxhunting art and artifacts. Many educational programs are available, including a tour of Civil War encampment sites within the park. The annual Three Day All–Breed dog show is held in September; the Morven Park Steeplechase Races are the second weekend in October. Open April through December; call or consult the website for hours during the restoration. 17263 Southern Planter Lane; (703) 777-2414; www.morvenpark.org.

Thomas Balch Library

For history buffs, there is no better place to start a Loudoun tour, especially if you have any family ties to the county. The map files, historical photograph selection, and house file provide an extensive introduction to Loudoun and the region. With a little planning and a phone call to the library, you and your small group can be treated to a brief history of the county by a member of the staff. Regular visitors to Loudoun have been known to schedule travel around the library's educational events. The building itself is an elegant example of Federal Revival architecture. Open daily; call or consult the website for hours. 208 West Market St.; (703) 737-7195; www.leesburgva.gov/services/library.

♨ EATING OUT, HANGING OUT

Blue Ridge Grill. Nine blocks from the center of town, this locally owned eatery serves American fare (steaks, seafood, pasta, and sandwiches). People who live here love the place. It faces Route 15 Bypass, but is accessed from Battlefield Parkway. Open daily, lunch and dinner. 955 Edwards Ferry Rd.; (703) 669-5505; www.brgrill.com.

Coffee Bean. Just up the hill from Gallery 222, makes for a relaxing pre- or post-gallery java break. 110 S. King St.; (703) 777-9556.

Downtown Saloon. Locals will likely always know the place as Payne's Biker Bar, but since 2001 it has had its current name. It is a casual, friendly place for a beer, directly across from the courthouse. As the sign in the window says: "Better here than across the street." Open late, of course. 7 N. King St.; (703) 669-3090.

Eiffel Tower Café. Madeleine Sosnitsky's Vienna, Va., restaurant, Pierre et Madeleine, has had a devoted following for many years. Since the opening of this Leesburg café in 1998, a new generation of French-enthused diners has found pleasure in the accordion-accompanied, inspired cuisine. 107 Loudoun St.; (703) 777-5142; www.eiffeltowercafe.com.

Galletta's Pasta & Italian Specialties. Featuring homemade pasta and Italian favorites for home cooking, Galletta's also features a limited menu of prepared foods, sandwiches, and salads. The lasagna and grilled-vegetable sandwich are known to create lines at the counter. Open daily, 11 to 6, Sundays until 2 p.m., closed Mondays. 211 Loudoun St. SE; (703) 737-3700; www.gallettas.com.

Leesburg Restaurant. A Leesburg landmark, the peanut soup and other southern favorites and traditional diner fare share the menu with commendable Caesar salads, soups, and desserts and shakes. Breakfast and a newspaper at the counter are hard to beat. Open from breakfast until 9 at night. 9 S. King St.; (703) 777-3292.

Lightfoot Restaurant. Located in a nineteenth-century bank building across from the courthouse, Lightfoot creates inventive renditions of nouvelle American cuisine. It is a destination restaurant—D.C. residents make the hour-long drive just for dinner. The piano bar upstairs overlooks the dining room on the "bank floor" downstairs. To dine at Lightfoot on a budget, head to the bar for a grilled-duck quesadilla or grilled-eggplant-and-plum-tomato sandwich—or the meatloaf. Open daily lunch and dinner. 11 N. King St.; (703) 771-2233; www.lightfootrestaurant.com.

Market Street Coffee. A coffee place that actually focuses on coffee, with a few pastries for dunking. Latte, cappuccino, and espresso freshly brewed for enjoyment at comfy chairs or small café tables. Check the website for poetry readings and open mike nights. Adjacent to the Talleyho Theatre. Open daily; open late Thursday through Saturday. 19 W. Market St.; (571) 258-0700; www.marketstreetcoffee.com.

Mighty Midget/B'z Barbecue. The Mighty Midget is a local favorite created out of an airplane fuselage. It is parked on Harrison Street, just across from Market Station. It has seen many incarnations over the years. B'z Barbecue, the business now inhabiting the can, has built a loyal following. Open regularly for lunch in the warm weather months (there are a few outside tables); or you can grab and go. 202 S. Harrison St.; (703) 777-6406.

Mom's Apple Pie Bakery. Located in the old tollhouse, Mom's is a Leesburg favorite. Memorable pies stuffed with homegrown and locally grown fruit, and an assortment of commendable cookies and breads. Take a pie home with you. 220 Loudoun St. SE; (703) 771-8590.

Puccio's New York Deli. Sub rolls you usually find only in the Wilmington/Philly-to-New York corridor (a slight crust, full of air), with ingredients worthy of the bread. The Balboa is a winner every time. Open for breakfast and lunch. 15 Loudoun St. SE; (703) 779-7676.

South Street Under. Panini, "ciapini" (a panini made on ciabatta bread), and assorted sandwich creations, along with memorable soups and salads, have made this local lunch spot a daily stop for many. For a few bucks, you can fill up on a hearty bowl of soup and fresh-baked bread. Located on the ground floor of Tuscarora Mill, there are tables outside and a few indoors. The gleaming lunch counter is the spot to sip soup and read a magazine. 205 South St. SE; (703) 771-9610.

Tuscarora Mill. Housed in a renovated grain mill, "Tuskie's" is the anchor of a much-touted collection of historic buildings known as Market Station, on Harrison Street. It's a warm place beneath the old mill rafters. Vegetarian favorites such as chestnut ravioli get the same attention from the chef as the rack of lamb. In the café, a.k.a., the bar, the fare is more casual. Open daily, lunch and dinner. 203 Harrison St.; (703) 771-9300; www.tuskies.com.

West Loudoun Street Cafe. The definition of a cozy lunch, an American delicatessen. A fine Rueben. Open daily for lunch. 7-A W. Loudoun St.; (703) 777-8693.

Loudoun County–an antique collector's dream. Photo: Courtesy of
Loudoun Convention and Visitors Association

🎁 DISTINCTIVE SHOPS AND STOPS

Antiques. If you are an antique hunter, you should plan to stay a
while. There are as many as a dozen shops in Leesburg.
For a brochure listing many of them, contact Loudoun
Convention & Visitors Association; (800) 752-6118;
www.VisitLoudoun.org. A couple of them are noted below
for their special offerings.

Black Shutter Antique Center. There are more than forty-five
dealers represented in the twenty rooms. For the antique-
averse browser, there is a terrific collection of literature
for young readers upstairs. *Robinson Crusoe, Heidi, Gulliver's
Travels, Rebecca of Sunnybrook Farm*—dozens of titles in
collector's editions from the 1930s through the 1960s.
There are signed first editions of Elmore Leonard and
other genre writers, too. Open daily till 5:30 (Sundays till
5:00). 1 Loudoun St.;(703) 443-9579;
www.blackshutterantiques.com.

Crème de la Crème. Colorful tableware and accessories from Europe; the majority is handcrafted in France, Italy, and Spain. Unique pottery, glassware, table linens, and serving dishes are featured. Open daily until 5. 101 S. King St.; (703) 737-7702; www.cdlcimport.com.

Ekster Antiques & Uniques. European imports for garden and home, with an emphasis on unique—even with the antiques. Features oversized patio planters, rattan divans, comfy chaises for the bedroom or porch, and arty home accessories. 101 S. King St.; (703) 771-1784; www.eksterantiques.com.

Gallery 222. This is an artist collaborative studio and gallery exhibiting a wide range of media, including printmaking, painting, sculpture, and photography. The gallery is home to Loudoun Academy of the Arts; classes for people of all ages and abilities are open to the public. Gallery open Monday through Saturday, 10 to 6. 222 S. King St.; (703) 777-8043; www.loudounacademy.org.

Gleedsville Gallery. A straightforward gallery offering original paintings and high-quality giclee prints of featured artists. While the work displayed spans the globe, this family-owned gallery is particularly dedicated to promoting the work of local and regional artists and subjects. 5 W. Loudoun St.; (707) 771-8055; www.gleedsvilleart.com.

Leesburg Antiques Emporium. Here you will find collections you otherwise wouldn't if you don't frequent the antiques shops: bins and bins of historical maps, botanicals, and prints on the first floor; downstairs are several cases of political campaign pins—DC political junkies could spend some serious time there. Open daily until 6. 32 S. King St.; (703) 777-3553; www.leesburgantiqueemporium.com.

Leesburg Vintner. This wine and cheese shop features an extensive inventory of Virginia wines. Mike Carroll and staff know them all, and they enjoy sharing what they know in a relaxed, no-nonsense way. 29 S. King St.; (703) 777-3322; www.leesburgvintner.com.

Market Station. A collection of seven historic buildings, including a log cabin from Maryland and the train depot from down the street. Each building displays a plaque describing its history. The Station contains restaurants, a natural foods store, and a spa. At Loudoun and Harrison streets.

Petite Dekor. So you left the kids at home to enjoy a weekend in a historic village—and enjoy yourself you have. With a gift from Petite Dekor, you can assuage those feelings of guilt at having left the kiddies behind. Toys, furniture, bedding, all kinds of things for kids, gifts for newborns, too. 22 W. Market St.; (703) 777-8245; www.petitedekor.com.

Rouge. In a creative re-use of a historic building, Rouge features a full-service day spa and store offering unique bath and body products. With a little planning, you can spend a Saturday exploring the historical attractions and schedule an afternoon massage before "fivesies" and dinner. In addition to all the lady's stuff, there is an extensive assortment of men's shaving and bath appurtenances. Open daily. 17 S. King Street; (703) 779-3700; www.rougespa.com.

⟪ LODGING

There are more than a dozen B&Bs in Loudoun County, but only a few in and near Leesburg. For others, see the Loudoun Scenic Drive itinerary in chapter 5, or consult www.VisitLoudoun.org or www.Loudounbandb.com.

Leesburg Colonial Inn. Ten rooms and suites in the heart of downtown. 19 S. King St.; (703) 777-5000; www.leesburgcolonialinn.com.

Norris House Inn. An elegant eighteenth-century inn restored to its original grandeur. 108 Loudoun St. SW; (703) 777-1806; www.norrishouse.com.

🚘 To Do Along the Way

Experience the Paranormal on a Leesburg Ghost Tour. Leesburg Ghost Tours have been written about widely as the only ghost tour guided by a trained paranormal investigator. Who knows who you will meet in some dark alley? It's entertaining and spooky. Tours leave nightly from the Georgetown Café, 11 S. King St. (703) 899-4994; www.vsra.net.

Paint Your Own Pottery at Imagine That. Bring a few friends, hang out, paint pottery, and catch up on old times; then move the conversation to a nearby café. Open Thursday through Sunday until 5. 14 Loudoun St. SE; (571) 258-1258; www.imaginethatleesburg.com.

Walk or Ride on the Washington & Old Dominion Trail. It's an easy bike ride to Purcellville along the scenic and famous W&OD. Or just take a stroll to walk off that fine Leesburg lunch.

Southern Loudoun

Driving south from Leesburg, the road primarily follows the route of the Old Carolina Road past the equestrian stables and farmland that are still integral to Loudoun County's rural economy. Four historic sites are spaced over the next ten miles. The first, Oatlands, about six miles south of town, may be Loudoun's best-known address.

Oatlands Historic District, which encompasses the area surrounding the Oatlands estate, is among the best preserved plantation landscapes along The Journey Through Hallowed Ground. At one time consisting of more than three thousand acres, the plantation was a self-contained village, complete with the tradesmen and staff to run and support an agricultural enterprise. Like other plantations of its time, it was dependent upon enslaved people to sustain it. Oatlands Plantation is the centerpiece of the historic district. Most of the site is owned or protected by easements by the National Trust for the Historic Preservation.

🏛 HISTORICAL SITES AND HERITAGE MUSEUMS

Oatlands Plantation

You could spend hours enjoying the grounds and visiting outbuildings without making it into the twenty-two-room Greek Revival mansion—but you will want to do that too. Built by George Carter beginning in 1804, Oatlands has its roots in the very founding of the nation—Carter was the great grandson of Robert "King" Carter, one of the

Oatlands Plantation.
Photo: Courtesy of Loudoun Convention and Visitors Association

most influential and wealthiest men of early Virginia. The greenhouse, built in 1810, is said to be the second oldest of its kind. The house is an architectural gem, and the array of programs offered at Oatlands could make a regular out of you. For gardeners and those of us who dream of hiring one, plan to spend a little quality time in the four-acre, terraced gardens. Oatlands also is home of the annual Loudoun Hunt Point-to-Point Races. Open Monday through Saturday, 10 to 5; Sunday, 1 to 5, March 30 through December 30. Located on Route 15, six miles south of Leesburg. (703) 777-3174; www.oatlands.org.

Church of Our Savior

The Episcopal Church of Our Savior, a simple brick structure erected in 1878, stands at the southern end of the district, set back from Route 15 on Oatlands Mill Road. A parish hall, built later, complements the scenic element of the picture. A small burial ground is adjacent to the church.

Mountain Gap School

The last one-room schoolhouse operating in Loudoun County, the school closed in 1953. It is located just north of the entrance to Oatlands, on the west side of Route 15. The grounds are accessible daily to wander, pump water from the old well, and peek into the windows of the school. A parking area for a few cars is located at the north end of the grounds. For tours, consult the Oatlands visitor center.

Before leaving the Oatlands vicinity, you can visit one of Loudoun's premiere nature preserves, located on a historic farmstead. Turn left just south of Oatlands onto Oatlands Mill Road. Beyond the Church of Our Savior, the road becomes The Woods Road, leading to Banshee Reeks.

Banshee Reeks

This lyrically named seven-hundred-acre nature preserve is well-known to area birders. It also is a historic nineteenth-century farm. In addition to the farmhouse, which has been restored as a visitor center, there is an 1830's log cabin and a bank barn. Hiking trails meander through fields and woods and along Goose Creek. In case you're wondering, the name combines two Gaelic words: a banshee is a female spirit; reeks is a word for hills. Sometime around 1840, the farm's Scots-Irish owner returned from an evening out and heard the mysterious cries of banshees in the reeks. The experience appears to have had a lasting impact. Open to the public the third weekend each month and for special programs. 21085 The Woods Road; (703) 737-7843; www.co.loudoun.va.us/prcs/parks/banshee.

————

Driving south from Oatlands, is the home of James Monroe, fifth president of the United States.

Oak Hill

This historically important site is not open to the public, but is worth knowing. James Monroe built it during his presidency. He is said to have retreated here to shape an idea first proposed by his Secretary of State, John Quincy Adams, to shield the Americas from European colonization and interference. Monroe formulated what we now call the Monroe Doctrine. In 1825, Monroe hosted Lafayette at Oak Hill. On this visit, Lafayette received the era's equivalent of a ticker-tape parade at every stop, including one at the Leesburg courthouse. Oak Hill was built by James Hoban, the Irish immigrant architect who was the designer and builder of the White House.

————

Further south, at the junction with Route 50, we come to Gilbert's Corner, named for the family that operated a gas station there beginning in the 1920s. At the time, the southbound highway ended here, hence a corner was formed. It was in 1941 that U.S. 15 was re-routed and extended north to Route 50.

From here, there are two more stops along the Journey in Loudoun County: Mt. Zion Church, a half mile east on Route 50, and Aldie Mills, a mile west on Route 50 in the village of Aldie.

Mount Zion Church

This was once on a crossroads; at this location, the Carolina Road crossed the Little River Turnpike, now Route 50. It is a serene spot, despite the proximity to the road. It wasn't always so. During the Civil War, Mount Zion was a battlefield, hospital, and prison. It was also a meeting place for John Mosby and his Rangers prior to raids. Later, it was a stopover point for Union soldiers. As a battle raged here, a correspondent died after being thrown from his frightened horse, becoming the only war reporter to die from injuries resulting from battle. In July 1864, Mosby's men clashed with Union Cavalry on church grounds.

The markers in the cemetery date to the early 1850s. Several Union and Confederate soldiers were buried here following the battle. Members of the black community, free and enslaved, were buried outside the walls. The Mount Zion Preservation Association hosts a number of events throughout the year. If you visit on days when the church is not open, there are interpretive brochures available at the site, and the windows are low enough to see the interior. Out on a sunny drive, this is a restful place to wander the cemetery and church grounds. Loudoun County Parks and Recreation; www.loudoun.gov/prcs/otherfac/mount.htm; (703) 777-0343. Also, Mount Zion Preservation Association; www.mtzioncpa.org

Aldie Mill and Aldie

Every kid loves the demonstrations and grinding tours at the mill. Adults do too. But the story of the mill and its founder make this more than a mill.

When twenty-nine-year-old Charles Fenton Mercer began construction in 1807, the area was practically a wilderness, but he knew that location was everything. Three years earlier he had chosen the site knowing that the Little River Turnpike would soon connect this very spot with Alexandria. Other turnpikes would lead here from the west. The operation he and a partner founded here would endure until the 1960s. Accompanying the mill were a distillery, sawmill, cooper, and wheelwright—everything a small mills' village needed to prosper.

Fenton was no mere miller. With the mill operated by a partner, then tenants, this Leesburg lawyer became engaged in state and national affairs. As a member of the House of Delegates, he was a leading advocate for creating public schools. In Congress, he promoted internal improvements such as roads and canals, serving as the first president of the C&O Canal. True to his anti-slavery sentiments, he was an originator of the failed idea to create the free state of Liberia. 39401 John Mosby Highway, Aldie; (703) 327-9777; www.aldiemill.org.

In the village of Aldie, there is a cluster of antique shops. Just beyond the mill is a bakery-café called the **Little Apple Pastry Shop**. They roast their own turkey on site and serve it up in sandwiches and platters. For "best pies along The Journey Through Hallowed Ground," the place has to rank. As does the apple bread pudding with rum sauce. For the road, buy a bag of country ham sandwiches on flaky biscuits.

On the west end of town is the **Little River Inn**. Lodgings include the B&B, a cozy cottage with living room and fireplace, and a two-bedroom log cabin, also with a fireplace. (703) 327-6742.

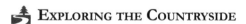

EXPLORING THE COUNTRYSIDE

Towns and Villages

Loudoun has several inviting small towns. Here are four close to Leesburg. To visit more, see the Loudoun Scenic Drive itinerary in chapter 5.

Hamilton. A little town with a lot of character, Hamilton was chartered in 1827. You can walk from end to end and back in about thirty minutes, enjoying the charming homes along the way. For natural foods and organic snacks, stop at Natural Mercantile on the east side.

Middleburg. Six miles west of Route 15 in Southern Loudoun, Middleburg is known far and wide for horses and foxhunting, It was founded in 1787, and thanks to those horses and the hunt, much of the land surrounding the town is still in pasture. In town are eateries and pubs, a bookstore, and two scoop shops—one serving up homemade ice cream. See Loudoun Heritage Loop for further description.

Purcellville. A railroad town along the Washington & Old Dominion, Purcellville is now the final stop on the W&OD Trail. It features a few antique shops and one of the world's finest thrift shops, plus a picturesque main drag lined with historic houses. With the "small plates" at Magnolia's at the Mill, you can live gourmand large on a budget. Speaking of large, the assortment of lagers, ales, and stouts on tap is worth walking out from Arlington on the W&OD—Dogfish Head and Smuttynose are just two of the dogs.

Waterford. It takes longer to describe this lovely little town than it does to drive there from Leesburg. Perhaps that is because the town is a National Historic Landmark and every building tells part of the town's story. It is an astonishingly well-preserved nineteenth-century village with roots dating back to the 1730s. Whereas many small towns along the Journey are captivating for their lively main streets, Waterford's appeal is that it is utterly quiet. For a livelier view of the town, check out the annual Waterford Fair. (See also Potomac Legacy Loop.) A self-guided walking tour is available at the Waterford Foundation office, Main and Second Streets. (540) 882-3018; www.waterfordva.org.

Waterford, Virginia. Photo: Kenneth Garrett.

Wineries

There are about a dozen wineries in Loudoun County. For a full listing, see www.visitloudoun.org/winecountry.cfm, or call (800) 752-6118 to request the Wine Trail Guide. Here is just a sampling of wineries on and near The Journey Through Hallowed Ground:

Breaux Vineyards. The Breaux family began producing wines as a hobby and realized that with a hit on their hands, it was time to produce commercially. The wines produced at the 404-acre estate have become some of Virginia's best known, as have the popular events. The annual Cajun weekend is one of the larger draws in the region. Located one mile from the intersection of Routes 9 and 761; (540) 668-6299; www.breauxvineyards.com.

Tarara Winery. The winery's setting on the Potomac and its special events are nearly as popular as its patio on the palisades. Spend some time in the tasting room or stroll along the six miles of hiking trails. 13648 Tarara Lane, Leesburg; (703) 771-7100; www.tarara.com.

Photo: CMW

Willowcroft Farm Vineyards. The awards bestowed upon Willowcroft have not changed the atmosphere at the winery. The working barn is more akin to a pick-your-own farm—laid back and personable. Willowcraft produces small quantities from the vineyard atop Catoctin Ridge, a nice place for a picnic and a walk too. 38906 Mount Gilead Rd., Leesburg; (703) 777-8161; www.willowcroftwine.com.

Windham Winery. The tasting room is in a barn set in a scenic valley. From the glass-enclosed porch grounds, you see beautiful views of a pond and Short Hill. There are twelve acres of vineyards on this five-hundred-acre farm, an inviting place for a picnic and to watch the birds from the deck. The cabernet franc is especially popular. 14727 Mountain Rd.; (540) 668-6464; www.windham winery.com.

Farms

Brossman's Orchard. This family-run farm specializes in peaches and nectarines, offering more than twenty-five varieties of pick-your-own or buy from the basket. Peaches, nectarines, sweet corn, tomatoes, melons, squash, and llopes. From Leesburg, take Route 15 north to Lucketts; turn right on Route 662 (Lucketts Road) at the traffic light and proceed 4.5 miles; take left at stop sign; entrance is first on right; 43975 Spinks Ferry Road. Daily, 10 to 6, July 1 through Labor Day. (703) 777-1127.

Crooked Run Orchard. Fruits and vegetables are grown without, or with a minimum use of, chemicals. Depending on the season, you can expect to find asparagus, sour cherries, gooseberries, thornless blackberries, white and yellow peaches, plums, pears, strawberries, and eleven varieties of apples. You can walk along the creeks or picnic in a quiet grove. From Route 7, turn left at Purcellville exit onto Route 287; turn right onto Business Route 7, E. Main Street; then take an immediate left at the first driveway for stand; turn left at second driveway for pick-you-own; 37883 E. Main St. The stand is open daily, 6 a.m. to 10 p.m. Pick-your-own hours are 8 a.m. to 6 p.m. Call for picking information; (540) 338-6642.

Farmer John's Wayside Stand. Produce is picked fresh every day; sweet corn is a specialty. During peach season, every week features a new variety of yellow or white peach. Yellow, paste, heirloom, and beefsteak tomatoes are abundant. Four types of

Photo: CMW

eggplant; many types of squash are available, too, as are fifteen varieties of apples in autumn. Five miles north of Leesburg on Route 15, 15520 James Monroe Highway. Daily, 7:30 a.m. until sunset, mid-June to mid-November. (703) 777 2100.

Great Country Farms. The market features pick-your-own or freshly picked berries, veggies, apples, and fruit in season. Admission is charged for the agri-tainment features such as a hayride, playing in the pumpkin patch, fishing in the pond, and playing on the sixty-foot slide. From Leesburg, take Route 7 west towards Winchester for sixteen miles; turn left on Route 760 into Bluemont; go left onto Snickersville Turnpike and then take the first right onto Foggy Bottom Road. Farm is a mile on the left; 18780 Foggy Bottom Rd., Bluemont. Open Tuesday through Sunday, 9 to 5, April through October. (540) 554-2073; www.greatcountryfarms.com.

Layngs Flower Farm. Loudoun's largest greenhouse operation offers spring pansies, Easter flowers, annuals, perennials, hanging baskets, herbs and vegetables, fall mums, cabbage and kale, fall pansies, poinsettias, Christmas trees. From Leesburg, take Route 15 south to Evergreen Mill Road, turn left; follow Evergreen Mill Road for seven miles. The farm is one mile past Ryan Road on left; 23520 Evergreen Mill Rd., Aldie. Open daily, 10 to 6. (703) 327-0872.

Outdoor Recreation

Blue Ridge Center for Environmental Stewardship. Adjacent to the Appalachian Trail, the Blue Ridge Center has nine-hundred acres and ten miles of hiking and equestrian trails. The remains of cabins and houses in the woods mark a farming settlement that existed until 1972. Harpers Ferry Road, two miles from U.S. 340. (540) 668-7640; www.brces.org.

Potomac Heritage Trail. A national scenic trail that connects Loudoun County with the Chesapeake Bay and Pittsburgh, Pa. Loudoun's segments follow the Potomac shoreline. Loudoun Parks and Recreation; www.Loudoun.gov/prcs.

Red Rock Wilderness Overlook. Just a couple miles from downtown Leesburg, this small park is a world apart from the growing suburbs nearby. Northern Virginia Regional Parks; www.nvrpa.org/redrock.

Rust Sanctuary. This sixty-two-acre preserve of the Audubon Naturalist Society was the home of Margaret Dole Rust, who bequeathed it as a nature center. Hiking trails pass through upland forest and meadows. The manor house now features a nature center. 802 Children's Center Road; (703) 669-0000.

Washington & Old Dominion Trail. You could ride out from Arlington on the W&OD and spend the weekend in Leesburg. Or you could walk along while in Leesburg, milkshake in hand, and ponder the idea of walking from Arlington to Leesburg. In Leesburg, the trail crosses South King Street one block from Loudoun Street. Northern Virginia Regional Parks; www.nvrpa.org/WOD.

Prince William County

TRAVEL ASSISTANCE

Prince William County/Manassas Convention & Visitors Bureau
14420 Bristow Road, Manassas; (800) 432-1792; www.visitpwc.com.

Manassas Visitors Center
9431 West Street; (877) 848-3018; www.visitmanassas.org.

Haymarket

With a nickname like "The Crossroads," it's easy to guess that geography was important to the town of Haymarket's founding and development. The junction of Old Carolina Road and the north branch of Dumfries Road, which connected the Shenandoah Valley with points east, formed the epicenter of town. It briefly served as a courthouse town in Virginia's old district court system. During the Civil War, the town was completely destroyed by fire at the hand of Federal troops, depriving it of its architectural history. Today, the town's new buildings are getting a lot of attention. The brick construction and historically sensitive designs are real winners, even if not totally accurate renditions of the old clapboard that once dominated the streets.

————

To visit Manassas Battlefield, follow Route 15 South to Route 234 (Sudley Road), turn left onto Route 234, or continue east on Route 55 one mile to Lee Highway, Route 29, and turn left. The battlefield is less than a mile ahead. Follow signs to the visitor center on Route 234.

Manassas Battlefield Military Park

The mere existence of this battlefield illustrates the idea of The Journey Through Hallowed Ground. That two major battles of the Civil War were fought here shows how significant the Piedmont has been in America's history. And the fact that beginning in 1940, five thousand acres have been preserved to commemorate the battles, shows that it is possible to safeguard the historic integrity of special places when people understand their importance.

For many people, the Battle of First Manassas remains one of the most intriguing days in U.S. history. With both sides expecting a war that would only last as long as the summer, the battle aroused a spectator's enthusiasm more akin to the Super Bowl than warfare.

Confederate General Thomas L. (Stonewall) Jackson, whose troops
routed the Union in the first Battle of Manassas, 1861.
Photo: Steven L. Spring

Picnickers and politicians took the train out from Washington to
watch the spectacle; they expected Union troops to win in a route
and continue on to Richmond. After the humiliating defeat, in which
Union soldiers running for their lives found their ways blocked by
retreating bystanders, it became clear that the war would long outlast
the ninety-day enlistment period of the troops.

A year later, the callow recruits of First Manassas were veteran
soldiers. Second Manassas would make the first battle seem like a
mere skirmish. The three-day carnage left 3,300 soldiers dead and
thousands more injured or missing. The Confederate victory,
considered a bold and brilliant victory by Robert E. Lee, set the
stage for the South to take the war onto Northern soil and to credibly
seek European recognition of the Confederate States of America.

Start your visit at the visitor center on Henry Hill. The exhibit
on First Manassas and a short film introduce the sites. Henry Hill
visitor center is on Sudley Road (Route 234). Open daily. (703) 754-
1861; www.nps.gov/mana.

Continue south on Sudley Road to visit historic Manassas.

Old Town Manassas

The railroad junction here was the object of desire that brought Northern and Southern generals into battle nearby. Today the station is the center of a lively dining and entertainment district in the old town, where you can find everything from burgers to fine dining. Interpretive signs along sidewalks and a museum near the train station guide you through the Civil War and its aftermath. The arts center, housed within a former candy factory a block from the depot, has a museum and art gallery. One of the big attractions, also at the depot, is the outdoor ice rink. The town visitor center is located in the train station, from which trains now ferry commuters into Washington.

—————

To return to the Journey's main route, follow Wellington Road northwest out of Manassas to Lee Highway. Turn left; Route 29 joins Route 15 in one mile, near **Buckland**. This little mill town was settled in the 1770s as a wagon stop and chartered in 1798 as Prince William County's first town in the Piedmont. In 1862, as Southern troops retreated from Manassas Junction, they were pursued by Union cavalry. Near Buckland, J.E.B Stuart lured the Northern troops into an ambush then scattered and chased them five miles over hills and creek beds, a skirmish known as the Buckland Races. At the historic village of Buckland are twenty-one vernacular buildings eligible for the National Register.Check the Buckland Preservation Society's Web site, www.bucklandva.org for information about visiting the site.

Buckland Mill, Broad Run.
Photo courtesy: Buckland Preservation Society

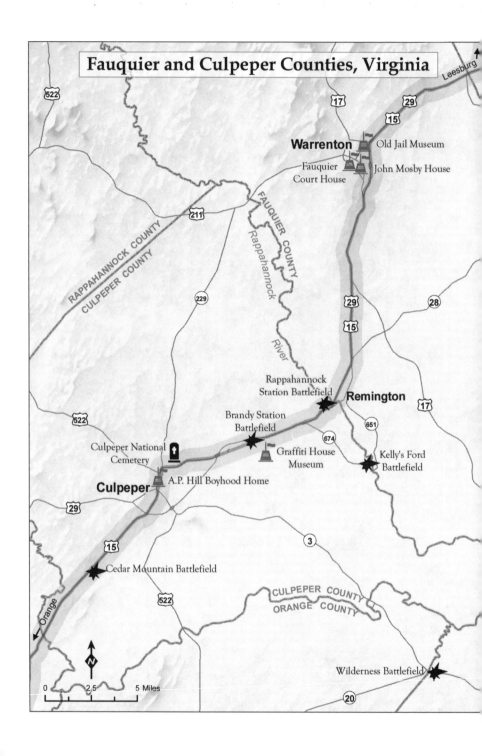

Fauquier and Culpeper Counties, Virginia

Leesburg

522

17

29

15

Warrenton   Old Jail Museum

Fauquier   John Mosby House
Court House

211

RAPPAHANNOCK COUNTY

CULPEPER COUNTY

FAUQUIER COUNTY

Rappahannock

229

River

29

15

28

Rappahannock
Station Battlefield   **Remington**   17

Brandy Station   651
Battlefield

522   674

Culpeper National   Graffiti House   Kelly's Ford
Cemetery   Museum   Battlefield

Culpeper   A.P. Hill Boyhood Home

29

15

3

Cedar Mountain Battlefield

522

CULPEPER COUNTY

ORANGE COUNTY

Orange

N

Wilderness Battlefield

0   2.5   5 Miles

20

—— Chapter 3 ——

The Journey Through
Fauquier and Culpeper Counties, Virginia

Distance: 43 MILES

HIGHLIGHTS ALONG THE JOURNEY THROUGH HALLOWED GROUND

Miles	Site
8	HISTORIC WARRENTON: FAUQUIER COUNTY COURT-HOUSE, JOHN MOSBY HOUSE, OLD JAIL MUSEUM
20	RAPPAHANNOCK STATION AND KELLY'S FORD BATTLEFIELDS
25	BRANDY STATION BATTLEFIELD, GRAFFITI HOUSE MUSEUM
31	HISTORIC CULPEPER: A.P. HILL BOYHOOD HOME, CULPEPER NATIONAL CEMETERY
37	CEDAR MOUNTAIN BATTLEFIELD

$\mathscr{I}$n Fauquier County, en route to Warrenton on Route 15, at nearly a mile a minute, you can be forgiven for a failure to notice the landmarks of time along the way, such as small stone houses tucked into narrow creek valleys or the distinctive Broad Run Baptist Church. To slow things down a bit, there are a few Civil War markers to draw your attention. One just north of Warrenton describes

Buckland Races, a Southern victory in a route that scattered Union cavalry over the surrounding hills.

Horses a gallop is an apt image for Fauquier and Culpeper counties. They'll tell you here this is horse country. Indeed, you're as likely to see a couple walking into lunch in boots and riding attire here as you are to see lycra-clad cyclists in Washington.

In Warrenton, you can slow down to a stroll, exploring the historic district on foot. You can do it in a wheelchair, too, thanks to the remarkably smooth and beautiful brick sidewalks the town has installed. Warrenton retains gems of its earliest architecture, including the early eighteenth-century jail, now the town's museum, and the famous Warren Green Hotel, now a municipal building.

The names associated with the town include the nation's founders. John Marshall, a young soldier with a Virginia regiment during the American Revolution, lived and practiced law here. He later became the fourth Chief Justice of the United States, after having served as a U.S. Representative and Secretary of State. Richard Henry Lee, signer of the Declaration of Independence, donated the land on which the courthouse stands.

South of Warrenton, en route to Culpeper, there is literally nowhere to cast an eye without spying a place where a Civil War battle or skirmish or encampment took place. Most of us tend to know the names of a few big battles; and folks who think of the conflict only as those battles sometimes wonder how the emotional power of the Civil War has endured. When you imagine hundreds of square miles occupied by young men living in tents, the continual movement of artillery and soldiers, and the way that every house of any size in these parts served as a hospital or boarding house, you begin to see. To the people who lived here, it was not unusual to see a five-hour line of soldiers and equipment move through a village—and you think *we have traffic!*

The Rappahannock River, on both sides, is the site of three battles—two of them encompassed several square miles. Brandy Station and Kelly's Ford were cavalry battles that are only now getting their full recognition as key battles in the war. At Brandy Station, there were some seventeen thousand cavalry horses engaged in the battle.

TRAVEL ASSISTANCE

Warrenton-Fauquier County Visitor Center
Maps, brochures, and information on local
attractions. Located behind the Mosby House,
173 Main St.; (540) 341-0988.

Warrenton and Fauquier County

Fauquier Chamber of Commerce
Listings of members and a wide variety of touring
destinations in the county.
www.fauquiercounty.gov/visitors.

The Partnership for Warrenton
Website provides information on visiting historic
downtown Warrenton.
www.historicwarrenton.org.

Culpeper

Culpeper Renaissance
233 E. Davis St., Suite 100;
(540) 825-4416;
www.culpeperdowntown.com

Culpeper Visitor Center. (The Train Station)
111 S. Commerce St.; (540) 727-0611;
www.visitculpeperva.org.

Culpeper—say it aloud like this: *Colpeppehr*. After you visit, you'll keep saying it in your mind, as in "I can hardly wait for my next visit to Colpeppehr." Custer loved it so much he went home to get married and brought his bride to live here during the Union occupation. It's a town with George Washington's fingerprints, too—he laid out the town in 1759. And it has another place in history: It is a story of how an old downtown reinvented itself into a vibrant, contemporary destination by focusing on its history and character. One merchant says this was possible because the town had good bones—it's also got soul.

Cedar Mountain is the southernmost heritage site along The Journey Through Hallowed Ground in Culpeper. That's a recent development. Not long ago you could only pause by the side of the road to glimpse the battle site. The Civil War Preservation Trust now owns important locations of the battlefield and welcomes the public to visit. Cedar Mountain was yet another instance of Stonewall Jackson grabbing victory from apparent defeat by rallying his troops at their moment of confusion and flight.

Old Town Warrenton

At the flower shop opposite the courthouse, in a building that was formerly the post office, if you wander in after school you might find three generations of one family working there. A few doors down at a specialty foods store, the former owner works for the current owner. Then there is the coffee shop that sells women's clothing, a tea room in a barber shop, and a quilting supply store in a carriage house where, one story goes, the resident ghost is a mare named Sophie. Warrenton is an altogether agreeable Southern town that seems to draw home its expatriates, who start businesses and pick up sharing the town yarns where their parents left off.

On slow days, you can tell the locals by watching them move from one conversation to the next down the sidewalk. Maybe that comes with the territory of a town that changed hands sixty-seven times during the Civil War—it takes time to keep up with the news of the day, after all. It's a town so amiable it's hard to imagine how anything ever gets done.

It's also the town that in the 1870s so antagonized its most famous hero, Colonel John Singleton Mosby, that he requested and accepted a diplomatic assignment in Asia to escape his neighbors. But that's another story. The brief cold shoulder shown to Mosby has long since warmed in the glow of history and his house in town is now being restored as a museum.

John Marshall, fourth Chief Justice of the United States, lived and worked here. Although his home no longer stands, a building he constructed for his son is now a jewelry store and art gallery.

And there is Extra Billy. A governor who served two terms twenty years apart, William Smith at one time ran a postal route from Washington, D.C., to Milledgeville, Georgia, at the time the state's capital. His scheme for developing spur routes and charging extra fees earned him the moniker Extra Billy Smith from a senator investigating federal waste. If anything, the name became a term of endearment for this popular general and politician.

Warrenton is a small enough town to comfortably walk its historic district in an hour or so. This leaves time to linger at your favorite buildings and visit the Old Jail Museum before lunch.

📖 WARRENTON WALKING TOURS

Warrenton Historic District

Warrenton is an altogether outstanding collection of historic structures in a range of styles and vintages. A walking tour brochure identifies many of them. The oldest home, called Paradise, was built for Colonel Martin Picket in 1758. More than thirty years after serving in the French and Indian War, Picket was a delegate in the Virginia Constitutional Convention of 1788. Also featured is the home of General William H.F. Payne, chief of the Black Horse Cavalry.

A Walking Tour of Warrenton, Virginia, published by the Fauquier Historical Society, is available a the visitor center, 173 Main Street; and at the Old Jail Museum next to the old courthouse.

🏛 HISTORICAL SITES AND HERITAGE MUSEUMS

Fauquier County Courthouse

Richard Henry Lee donated seventy-one acres for the county seat, including the site of the courthouse. He chose the site after determining the highest point in town, a decision which complements the extraordinary views from the courthouse steps. Fires destroyed structures built in 1790, 1814, and 1854. The current 1890 building is a virtual reproduction of the 1854 structure. A painting of Chief Justice Marshall hangs in the courtroom. Twice it was

Fauquier County Courthouse. Photo: Mike DeHart

rescued and removed from the courthouse. The first time was during the Civil War, when a local man, concerned that approaching Yankees might sack the town, used a pocket knife to remove it. The second time, during an election celebration in which a bonfire got out of control, a couple of Warrenton teens saved the portrait.

John Mosby House

Known as Brentmoor when built for Judge Edward M. Spilman, 1859-61, the home was purchased by John Singleton Mosby in 1875. Mosby made an attempt at a quiet life in the practice of law in Warrenton. Despite his heroics in the Civil War as the commander of the cavalry known as Mosby's Rangers, townspeople could not forgive his support of Grant in the election of 1872. In 1878, he accepted a diplomatic post in Hong Kong, then later served as an assistant U.S. Attorney. He died in 1916 in Washington, D.C. His home in Warrenton has been restored with plans to open it as the John Singleton Mosby Museum. 173 Main Street; www.mosbymuseum.com.

Old Jail Museum

The original jail was built in 1808, but by 1823 a larger structure and a home for the jailer were needed. A two-story building behind the old jail was built, and the Old Jail was converted to a residence. The jail operated until 1966. The original building is now a museum of local history. In the rear building is a the old solitary confinement lock-down and other jail exhibits. Located next to the Old Courthouse; (540) 347-5525.

Virginiana Room, Fauquier County Library

The local history collection houses titles highlighting regional history, biographies of notable Virginians, a meticulously organized array of articles, Works Project records from the 1930s, and periodicals dating to 1865.

The Old Jail Museum, Warrenton. Photo: Mike DeHart

Open daily (1 to 5 p.m. on Sundays). 11 Winchester St.; (540) 347-8750.

Warren Green Hotel

Urban renewal claimed a large portion of this imposing building, but the part that remains is still a gem. A lobby exhibit charts the Who's Who of people who dined or stayed here at the 1819 Norris Tavern or its successor, the Warren Green. General Lafayette and James Monroe dined here during Lafayette's 1825 American tour. Henry Clay declared his presidential candidacy from the porch; General George McClellan bade his men farewell from that same porch after President Lincoln sacked him; Andrew Jackson stayed twice. The original Norris building burned in 1876. To many American Anglophiles, it will always be known as the home of Wallis Warfield. She lived here while awaiting her decree of divorce from Ernest Simpson so that she could marry King Edward, who abdicated the throne to marry her. The building houses county offices and is open to the public during business hours. 14 Hotel St.

Photo: Ed Lehmann

Warrenton Cemetery

The final resting place for Colonel John Mosby and other notable Warrenton figures, the cemetery also holds the remains of six hundred Confederate soldiers who fought at Manassas. During one of the thirty-odd Federal occupations of Warrenton, Union troops stole the wooden crosses marking the Confederate dead for use as firewood. For many years after, the graves were marked simply as unknowns. Decades later, a researcher chasing a lead on another topic came across the names of all the soldiers buried here. Their names are now inscribed on a memorial.

☕ EATING OUT, HANGING OUT

Claire's at the Depot. The building is a splendid example of the reuse of a historic structure. This classic brick stationhouse was built in 1908 to replace a wooden structure from the mid-1850s. Claire's is more than a pretty building. Chef Sandy Freeman's menu, while gathering up tastes from around the world, for old time's sake includes a couple contemporary takes on old Southern favorites, such as cornmeal crusted Chesapeake fried oysters and she-crab soup. The bar in front is a pleasant place to end an afternoon of sightseeing. 65 S. Third St.; (540) 351-1616; www.clairesrestaurant.com.

The Earthly Paradise. If you know poet William Morris, you get it right away. "The idle singer of an empty day." It's coffee; it's clothing; don't try to figure it out; have a cappuccino instead. 31 Main St.; (540) 341-7115.

Jimmie's Market/Madison Tea Room. One of the oldest businesses on Main Street, under current ownership since 1975, Jimmie's sells gourmet meats, cheeses, groceries, and an assortment of wines. In the old barber shop next door, a tea room serves classic Southern tea. 24 Main St.; (540) 347-2631

Main Street Bistro. A quiet place serving casual American fare, sandwiches, salads, and soup. A nice place to take a book and order up the soup. Kid friendly, too. 32 Main St.; (540) 428-1778.

Molly's Irish Pub. The pub masquerades as a family restaurant during the day. It is kid-welcoming for lunch and early evening before giving way to music and the night life. It's also smoke-free until 3 p.m. Lamb stew and fried cod, curry and chips mix it up with Irish-named American dishes. 36 Main St.; (540) 349-5300; www.mollysirishpub.com.

Natural Marketplace. Grab picnic fixings at the grocery or belly up to the deli and juice bar for an inventive menu of salads, spreads, and sandwiches—organic and flavorful. Organic meats plus yummy vegetarian selections like goat cheese with roasted tomatoes and Kalamata spread, or grape leaves and tahini sauce. 5 Diagonal St.; (540) 4111; www.thenaturalmarketplace.com.

Renee's Gourmet to Go. Prepared right; priced right. Just what a lunch counter ought to be. Good soup, too. 15 S. Third St.; (540) 347-2935.

Smokey Joe's Café. You guessed right. Savory Southern-style cooking and barbecue, with traditional fare such as burgers and salads. Get there. Open daily for lunch and dinner. Saturday for breakfast, lunch, and dinner. 11 Second St.; (540) 341-0102.

✠ Distinctive Shops and Stops

The Bead Shoppe. A Wednesday afternoon and more than a dozen people are, what, shopping for beads? It's true. Ladies (mostly) stopping on their way to and from everywhere detour here for all the supplies they need to bead. Local moms and their daughters, too. If you bead, this is your place. Open daily. 43 Main St.; (540) 347-5530; jwww.oldtownbeads.com.

Berkley Gallery. One of only a few purist galleries along the Old Carolina Road, Berkley exhibits original paintings and sculptures and limited-edition photographs. There is enough from the Piedmont and Chesapeake as befits a Virginia gallery, but the art and artists cover a much wider geography and perspective. Open daily. 40 Main St.; (540) 341-7367; www.berkleygallery.com.

Christine Fox. You don't usually think of driving to a small town to find the fashions of New York or Paris, but that's what the line of customers from DC claim as their aim. (Author confesses the inability to distinguish a Longchamp handbag but appreciates the effect). 47 S. Third St.; (540) 347-3868.

Designs by Teresa. An arty flower shop in the former post office, with a room full of teddy bears up the spiral staircase. They share that second floor room with a ghost named Annie, so everyone says. 7 Main St.; (540) 342-4762.

Horse Country Saddlery. Not your ordinary tack shop. In addition to all the accoutrements an equestrian might need, you'll find men and women's clothing, hats, gloves, and belts, some home décor items, and a fascinating collection of books. 60 Alexandria Pike; (540) 347-3141.

Marta von Dettingen. A jewelry store and gallery, the structure was built by Chief Justice John Marshal for his son as a confectionary shop. After an eight-year restoration effort, von Dettingen opened the shop in 2003, featuring estate jewelry, silver jewelry, oil paintings and prints, cameo glass, bowls, and lamps. Oh, and chocolates, too, to honor the building's history. Open Monday through Saturday. 56 Main St.; (540) 347-7670.

Mom's Apple Pie. A Warrenton location for this Loudoun County institution. Fourth-generation owners who bake memorable pies and cakes using as many homegrown ingredients as possible. Open daily. 22 Waterloo St.; (540) 347-2075.

Shelf Life. Contemporary hip takes on classic furniture styles with an emphasis on functionality, with many of them in compact designs ideal for the smaller rooms of historic houses and apartments. 52 Main St.; (540) 349-7706.

Town Duck. Features specialty food items, such as cheeses and wines, chocolates and caviar. Also on the shelves are painted glass, crystal glasses and goblets, and pottery and ceramics by local potters. Open daily until 5 (Sunday till 4); 15 Main St;. (540) 347-7237; www.townduck.com.

The Virginia Company. The popular catalogue company has a retail store on Main Street, featuring Virginia hams, sausages, peanuts, wines, souvenirs, and other Old Dominion things. 88 Main St.; (540) 341-1951.

⌂ LODGING

Black Horse Inn. There are nine distinctive guestrooms, some with fireplaces and whirlpool baths, a handsome drawing room and quiet sitting room, and incredible views. This is a special occasion place, but a few of the rooms are priced comparably to nearby motels—no real decision there. Enjoy a late afternoon tea on the spacious, sunny porch, followed by a stroll to the stables before the sun sets. Just outside Old Town Warrenton at 8393 Meetze Rd. (540) 349-4020; www.backhorseinn.com.

Highland Farm Inn. About ten minutes from Warrenton on thirty-six acres in horse country, the house is on the eighteenth-century estate of Hancock Lee. In addition to rooms in the main house, the old stone kitchen has been converted to a guest cottage. A peaceful, quiet location to hang out by the pond, take a walk and watch the horses, or swim in the pool. 10981 Lee's Mill Rd., Remington. (540) 439-0088; www.highlandfarminn.com.

Inn at Kelly's Ford. About ten minutes from Warrenton, this country inn and conference center is located at the site of the Battle of Kelly's Ford. Accommodations include cottages with suites, two rooms in the main house, and two houses available for exclusive use. Walk the grounds to Kelly's Ford, enjoy the outdoor pool, have dinner in the pub, and stay for music on Friday and Saturday evenings. 16589 Edwards Shop Rd., Remington. (540) 399-1779; www.innatkellysford.com.

Exploring the Countryside

Wineries

Pearmund Cellars. You can practically earn a PhD in grape growing hanging out in the tasting room—no studying or papers to write, though. A true, craft wine operation. The Chardonnays and Ameritage are noted by wine lovers as among the region's finest. Open daily. 6190 Georgetown Rd., Broad Run. (540) 347-3475; www.pearmundcellars.com.

Rogers Ford Farm Winery. Come for a tasting and spend the weekend in the cottage—one of the few vineyards in the area to have a B&B operation. The Petit Verdot and Jacob Christopher Chardonnay are two of the most popular offerings. Rogers Ford Road, Sumerduck. (540) 439-3707; www.rogersfordwine.

Outdoor Recreation

C.M. Crockett Park. The Germans who settled the area had a quarry operation here; all that remains is the lake, which makes for fine birding. The trails in the hundred-acre wood (no kidding) are home to cedar waxwings, eastern phoebes, and a variety of songbirds. South of Warrenton on the Virginia Birding & Wildlife Trail, Culpeper Loop. www.dgif.state.va.us/wildlife/vbwt.

Remington Bicycle Trails. The tiny town of Remington, adjacent to Route 15 just north of the Rappahannock River, is the starting point for a series of bicycle loops on the back roads of Southern Fauquier County and Northern Culpeper County. Parking is available across from the deli, and a trailhead kiosk map illustrates the route. www.remingtonva.org.

Whitney State Forest. Just south of Warrenton on Lees Ridge Road, the 147-acre forest has six miles of trails for hiking and biking. On the Virginia Birding & Wildlife Trail, Culpeper Loop. www.dgif.state.va.us/wildlife/vbwt.

Photo: CMW

Wildcat Mountain Natural Area. Seven miles west of Warrenton
off Route 211, altitudes range from 500 to 1,200 feet over
more than 600 acres of woods. There are stands of huge
oak and hickory mixed with stands of pine and younger
forest. The area was settled and farmed into the twentieth
century. A Virginia family donated land to the Nature
Conservancy, which has added to the preserve over the
years. http://nature.org/wherewework/northamerica/
states/virginia/preserves/art1247.html

———

Driving south from Warrenton, you can weave your way
toward the Rappahannock River by following Meetze Road
to Meetze, then turning right on Green Road, which
becomes Bowers Run Road. You'll have to get on Route
17 for a mile, then take Remington Road west into town
of Remington.

Remington. Known during the Civil War as Rappahannock Station,
the area surrounding town was of great interest to both
sides due to its proximity to nearby river fords. It's a tiny,
quiet place with a few treats. It is the hub of a network of
bicycle routes. A deli and market across from the trailhead
sells earthy crunchy things and dried beans and grain in
bulk, as well as local meats, cheeses, and treats. At the
pharmacy, you can enjoy a milkshake at the counter.
Remington also is the apex of the triangle of three Civil
War battles that took place within a few miles.

Three Battles of the Rappahannock

The more you travel the region, the more the realization hits you
that many battles of the Civil War were fights over the same territory
time and again. The three battles are separated by only several
months and a few miles. For each, the Rappahannock River was
the dividing line of battle. They are presented here in their order

along the Journey north to south, rather than chronologically. To move along the roads traveled by the troops, take Sumerduck Road from Remington to Kelly's Ford, then Kelly's Ford Road back toward Route 15.

🏛 HISTORICAL SITES AND HERITAGE MUSEUMS

Rappahannock Station

Now the town of Remington, this hamlet on the Rappahannock is just north of the fields General Robert E. Lee had chosen to winter his army in 1863, after sparring their way south following July's defeat at Gettysburg. On November 7, George Meade's Federal troops crossed the river and fell into Lee's carefully laid plan to repulse them. Inexplicably, Lee's generals failed to execute according to plan and sustained heavy losses—including the loss of the bridgehead Lee had planned to use for his own attack. It was a humiliating defeat. That night, he marched his army south.

Although much of the battlefield is privately owned, there are interpretive signs and a self-guided walking tour that can be downloaded from www.nps.gov/frsp/rapp.htm.

Kelly's Ford

Both sides wintered on opposites sides of the Rappahannock River in 1862. There were occasional skirmishes and cavalry raids, more to break the monotony than to gain any real advantage. Also on opposing sides of the river were two friends and West Point classmates, Union Brigadier General William Averell and Confederate Brigadier General Fitzhugh Lee. Through messengers they taunted one another, with Lee "inviting" Averell to visit and bring a sack of coffee. The morning of March 17, 1863, saw the battle known as the first real fight between two cavalries east of the Mississippi. Considered a Southern victory, the battle resulted in a loss that shook the Confederacy. A young artilleryman and hero of the Battle of Fredericksburg, John Pelham, died in the battle. At twenty-four, he had already achieved a mythical status. His death caused mourning through the Confederacy; his body lay in state in Richmond following his death. Averell, upon his retreat, left behind a sack of coffee for Lee.

The battlefield is intact and open to the public at Chester Phelps Wildlife Management Area, accessed from Remington via Sumerduck Road, or by Kelly's Ford Road from Route 15, south of Remington. For self-guided tour, download at www.nps.gov/frsp/kelly.htm. You can also visit the battlefield from the Inn at Kelly's Ford, which hosts reenactments; www.innatkellysford.com.

Brandy Station and Graffiti House

The largest cavalry battle fought in North America wasn't really supposed to happen. It was June 9, 1863. Lee was

Signatures found beneath layers of paint in the aptly named Graffiti House. Photo: Steven L. Spring

taking the war north into Pennsylvania and directed J.E.B. Stuart to conduct a day of maneuvers as a way of screening his army's northward march up the Shenandoah Valley. Union Major General Hooker thought the Confederates were preparing a raid, so ordered an attack, resulting in seventeen thousand horsemen in battle.

There is a self-guided driving tour of the battlefield available at Graffiti House in Brandy Station. Graffiti House is owned and operated by the Brandy Station Foundation, which, along with the Civil War Preservation Trust, has helped preserve about one thousand acres of the Brandy Station Battlefield. Graffiti House is named for the dozens of signatures, sayings, and other missives found beneath layers of paint in the house that had been a hospital and, most likely, a boarding house for wintering soldiers. Graffiti House is a special little museum. In addition to the charcoal signatures on the walls, artifacts have been donated by descendents of soldiers who have visited the house. One wall downstairs invites descendents to sign beneath their kin's name. Ask to see the Stuart family wall with signatures of the general's descendents.

From Route 15/29, a few miles north of Culpeper, exit left at the sign for Brandy Station. Graffiti House is at the end of the road. Open year-round on Wednesdays and Saturdays. Additional summer hours on Fridays and Sundays. Closed on major holidays. www.Brandystation foundation.org. Also, www.nps.gov/frsp/brandy.htm.

———

From Graffiti House, travel south on Brandy Road, which becomes Business 15/29 and leads into downtown Culpeper. As ever, the visitor center is a good place to start. Turn left onto E. Davis and go two blocks to the train station, which houses a delightful visitor's center.

Fireman's Parade, Culpeper, Virginia.
Photo: Courtesy of Culpeper Renaissance, Inc.

Culpeper

By the time he was commissioned to survey and plat the town then known as Fairfax, the twenty-seven-year-old George Washington had already risen to the rank of major and distinguished himself in the French and Indian War. The year was 1759. Only sixteen years later, heeding the call of the Virginia Convention to organize a militia that could be put into action at a minute's notice, men of Fauquier, Culpeper, and Orange counties organized as the Culpeper Minutemen. They participated in the Battle of Great Bridge in December 1775, which led three weeks later to an assault on Norfolk that effectively booted the British from power in the Virginia colony.

Because the train depot's value as a supply line attracted attention from both Union and Confederate armies, Culpeper saw much fighting and destruction of property during the Civil War. There were more than a hundred battles and skirmishes in around the town. It is a town with colorful stories related to each army's occupation. Nothing brings these stories to life like a guided walking tour (see Tours).

Like many a town, big or small, Culpeper's downtown endured a period of boarded shops while in transition from a place to buy feed and farm implements into one to buy furnishings and decorative items reminiscent of farm life. Culpeper's renaissance has brought an international flare rivaling much larger cities—while retaining its small town character. Within the two blocks of East Davis street are three fine restaurants featuring French and European cuisine, a French chocolatier, a shop featuring Mexican-made boots and jackets crafted with Spanish leather, and a boutique specializing in aboriginal and international gifts and clothing, not to mention an international gourmet shop. And that's just on one block. On South Main Street are notable restaurants featuring European and Thai cuisine.

That's not to say that Virginia has vanished. Country ham, country cooking, and country antiques are alive and well in Culpeper. In a taste of the new Old Dominion, there is a market featuring organic meat, poultry, cheese, and dairy products all grown nearby.

Culpeper County Courthouse.
Photo: Steven L. Spring

📖 CULPEPER WALKING TOURS

Guided Civil War Walking Tour of Culpeper by Virginia Morton. The author of the novel *Marching Through Culpeper* is a seasoned story-teller, as entertaining as she is knowledgeable. A lot of fun for a group of friends and family. By appointment only. (540) 825-9147; www.edgehillbooks.com.

In & Around Culpeper: Walking and Driving Tours. A booklet available free of charge at the visitor center, at the end of E. Davis St.

🏛 HISTORICAL SITES AND HERITAGE MUSEUMS

A.P. Hill Boyhood Home

Ambrose Powell, who went by the name Powell, grew up in a prominent Culpeper family. The older front portion of the home dates to 1774. The Hill family carried out extensive renovations on the home during the 1850s. A plaque on the Davis Street side of the home provides information about A.P. Hill's time in Culpeper and the war. 102 N. Main.

Burgandine House. Photo: Steven L. Spring

Culpeper National Cemetery. Photo: Steven L. Spring

Burgandine House

This log and plank cabin is Culpeper's oldest house. It was a country cabin when Culpeper County was established in 1749, long before the town grew up to meet it. It is on the grounds of the Museum of Culpeper History. It is listed on the National Register of Historic Places.

Culpeper National Cemetery

This Civil War-era cemetery was established in 1867 to inter soldiers who died in the Culpeper area. The flagpole at the high ground was also the position from which Confederate artillery fired on Union soldiers at the depot in the Battle of Culpeper Station. Take U.S. Avenue from East Street to 305. (540) 825-0027

Hill Mansion

This Italian villa-style mansion was the home of E.B. Hill, brother of General A.P. Hill. It was used as a Confederate hospital, then later as a Union headquarters (with the Hill family relegated to two rooms). Robert E. Lee visited his son, Rooney, here as he was recovering from wounds received at the Battle of Brandy Station. Built in 1854, it is

Hill Mansion. Photo: Steven L. Spring

listed on the National Register and remained in the Hill family until 1990.

Museum of Culpeper History

Dinosaurs tracking through Culpeper! Of course, this occurred before the existence of Culpeper. Come see the tracks. Then you can visit history of a more recent vintage, from a replica American Indian village to exhibits on the founding of Virginia, the development of the first suburban shopping center, and the Iran hostage crisis. Open Monday through Saturday, 9 to 5. 803 S. Main St.; (540) 829-1749; www.culpepermuseum.org.

Railroad Depot

This attractive station was built in 1904 to replace the station built in 1854. The Battle of Culpeper Courthouse, in September 1863, was fought at and around the station. The flamboyant General George Custer had his horse shot from under him here. The station is served today by Amtrak and houses the Culpeper visitor center. The station also is home to a local arts organization that manages gallery space featuring regional artists throughout the building. 109 S. Commerce St., (540) 825-8628. www.culpepervachamber.com

☕ EATING OUT, HANGING OUT

Ala Heart Café. Don't let the name frighten you. Even though it is suggestive of a coronary patient's cafeteria, the food is fresh and tasty. In a town full of European country cuisine and Virginia country cooking, here there is a focus on salads, yummy vegetarian selections, and wraps. And there are tasty takes on traditional fare like roast beef sandwiches and chicken salad—less salt, more herbs. 106 W. Cameron St.; (540) 727-9332.

Baby Jim's Snack Bar. It's where the locals go for burgers, hot dogs, and milkshakes. 701 N. Main St.; (540) 825-9212.

Bella-Mia's Italian American Deli. The Italian sandwiches feature premium meats and cheeses and fresh ingredients. The menu also includes a few hot entrees and Italian specialty items. 128 N. Main St.; (540) 727-7632.

Cameron Street Coffee. Were it not for the exceptional roasts (which you can watch and smell in process) and the good sandwiches, you would still have to visit just to see this memorable adaptive use of an old warehouse. Bring a book and head upstairs to the loft. Open daily. 110 E. Cameron St.; (540) 829-9581.

Dee Dee's Family Restaurant. The country breakfast in the morning and the pit barbecue in the afternoon is really as far as you need to go on this menu, but there are lots of home-cooked dishes to choose. 502 N. Main St.; (540) 825-4700.

Foti's. Culpeper's trendy pick is the invention of three restaurateurs who earned their stripes at the Inn at Little Washington, to which they pay homage but don't attempt to copy. A Mediterranean influence and a bit of adventure, with the vegetarian fare getting the same imaginative attention as other dishes. 219 E. Davis St.; (540) 829-8400; www.fotisrestaurant.com.

Frost Café. Put some coins in the jukebox and order up something from the grill; follow it up with a shake and some pie. Family dining. 101 E. Davis St.; (540) 825-9212.

Hazel River Inn, Copper Kettle Soup Bar, The Pub. There are three eateries in the old hardware store, all notable within their niche. The soup bar is quaint and casual, and the soups—let's just say there are ways to lick a bowl in public without drawing attention. The pub serves up memorable renditions of your average tavern fare, but with bottles of Hacker Pschorr and Urqell, and evening music. Upstairs in the main restaurant, the Piedmont bison is true local fare. 195 E. Davis St.; (540) 825-7148; www.hazelriverinn.com.

It's About Thyme. You almost wish for a downpour outside for the excuse to linger a little longer over lunch of, say, boar sausage over salad greens or smoked chicken ravioli. Or just to dip fresh rosemary bread into a cup of carrot jalapeno soup and gaze at the mural-painted wall of a village day. The cuisine is European country. All the pastas are fresh made; the desserts a worthy finish. 128 E. Davis St.; (540) 825-4264.

Lucio. Not all of Culpeper's inspired cuisine is up town. Former White House chef Lucio Tonizzo's restaurant features European cuisine in a charming setting within one of Culpeper's historic houses. 702 S. Main St.; (540) 829-9788.

Thai Culpeper Restaurant & Bar. With the success of this cuisine in the Virginia suburbs of D.C., Northern Virginians have high expectations when it comes to Thai. No disappointments here. 401 S. Main St.; (540) 829-0777.

✣ DISTINCTIVE SHOPS AND STOPS

Ace Books & Antiques. The promo says more than 250,000 used books, and from the look of the stacks that seems low. A huge selection of paperback fiction, but also a wide assortment of hardcover nonfiction, including history, biography, social criticism, and science. Closed Monday. 120 W. Culpeper St.; (540) 825-8973.

Another Dimension. Artwork covering a range of traditions and styles by local artists and craftspeople from around the world, including costume jewelry, paintings, fabric toys, handbags, clothing, and artifacts. Closed Sunday and Monday. 172 E. Davis St.; (540) 829-9062; www.anotherdimensiononline.com.

Calhoun's Country Hams. The name says it all. Tom Calhoun is famously known as the "ham man" for his generations' old curing recipes. Open daily. 219 S. East St.; (540) 825-8319; www.calhounhams.com.

Cameleer. A veritable amusement park of international gifts, clothing, outerwear, aboriginal art, crafts, and other imaginative decorator items for the home. 125 E. Davis St.; (540) 825-8073.

The Castaway Company. A full-line Orvis dealer offering fly-fishing supplies, outdoor apparel, and artwork. Castaway also teaches classes and organizes group fishing instruction and expeditions. Open daily; closed Sunday in winter. 254 E. Davis St.; (540) 829-5311; www.thecastaway company.com.

Chateau du Reaux. Features sauces, cheeses, pates and spreads, wines—you get it—from around the world. There also is an extensive assortment of food and wine from Virginia. 219 E. Davis St.; 540-829-WINE; www.culpeperwines.com.

Great antiques. Photo: Culpeper Renaissance, Inc.

Food for Thought. A feast of locally grown, natural meats and dairy products, including grass-fed beef, pastured lamb, pork, and poultry. A rare treat too, local craft cheeses. 202 E. Davis St.; (540) 727-9525.

Frenchman's Corner. A fine European chocolatier and bakery also offering selected cheeses of the world. Bread, cheese, chocolate . . . go early enough in the day to get some bread. Open daily. 141 E. Davis St.; (540) 825-8025; www.frenchmanscorner.com.

Janal Leather. Imported leather paddock boots and riding boots (this is horse country, after all), along with footwear, jackets, purses. And, designer cowboy boots, of course. 102 E. Davis St.; (540) 829-5590. www.janalleather.com.

Sara Schneidman Gallery. The gallery focuses on Sara Schneidman's unique, colorful art, pottery, rugs, and dis-tinctive stationery products. Closed Sunday and Monday. 122 East Davis St.; (540) 825-0034; www.saraschneidman.com.

⊟ LODGING

Fountain Hall B&B. With an in-town location, you can park once and spend your time wandering the historic streets. Or leave the car at home and arrive by train. The magnificent Colonial Revival stands on ground once owned by Alexander Spotswood, Virginia's colonial governor. The inn has six rooms, some with private balconies, whirlpools or suites. 609 South East St.; (540) 825-8200; www.fountainhall.com.

Hazel River Inn. About seven miles from downtown Culpeper on five peaceful acres. A heated in-ground pool in the garden is a pleasing spot from which to gaze at the Blue Ridge. Take a walk in the woods and return to the fire. Owned by the proprietors of the Culpeper restaurant of the same name, so continental breakfast means smoked salmon. 11227 Eggbornsville Rd.; (540) 937-5854; www.hazelriverinn.com.

🚗 TO DO ALONG THE WAY

Float or Paddle on the Rapidan or Rappahannock. Let Rappahannock River Campground handle the details; all you have to do is float. (540) 399-1839; www.canoecamp.com.

Take a Fly-fishing Excursion with Friends. You and your buds can get an exclusive day on a private stretch of river, complete with lessons, tackle, food, and drink. See the Castaway in Culpeper.

Take a Guided Walk through Culpeper. A Civil War tour of Culpeper brings history to life. See Culpeper Walking Tours.

Thrill to the Steeplechase at the Virginia Gold Cup. This world renowned event takes place in May and October at Great Meadow. Stop by the Gold Cup office on Main Street, Warrenton. (549) 347-2612; www.vagoldcup.com.

Tour a Moonshine Distillery. See the home of Virginia Lightening. Belmont Farms Distillery makes corn whiskey in a copper pot still, like it's been done since the earliest days of America. 13490 Cedar Run Rd., Culpeper; (540) 825-3207; www.virginiamoonshine.com.

Walk the Rail-trail from Warrenton. Take a morning walk or ride along the path leading from the Old Depot in Warrenton.

 EXPLORING THE COUNTRYSIDE

Wineries

Old House Vineyards. The name reflects the laid-back character of the estate, a pleasing stop in the country. Winemaker Doug Fabbioli, formerly of Tarara, is one of the better-known Commonwealth vintners. 18351 Corky's Lane, Culpeper. (540) 423-1032; www.oldhousevineyards.com.

Prince Michel Vineyards. Winemaker Brad Hansen is recognized as one of Virginia's most learned and experienced at his craft. Wines are produced under the labels Prince Michel, Rapidan River, and Madison. Route 29, Leon. (540) 547-9720; www.princemichel.com.

Outdoor Recreation

Mountain Run Lake Park. Located on the lake of the same name, the setting is the scenic hills of western Culpeper County. Only fifteen minutes from downtown Culpeper, there are dramatic views of the Blue Ridge Mountains. Take a picnic lunch. Go south on Route 29 to Mountain Run Lake Road.

Yowell Meadow Park. This park is actually in town, but it has a delightful one-mile nature trail that passes a monument to the Culpeper Minutemen.

🏛 HISTORICAL SITES

Rapidan Historic District. This tiny hamlet straddles the Rapidan River and the counties of Orange and Culpeper. The star attractions are two Carpenter Gothic churches: the lovely Emmanuel Episcopal on the Culpeper side of the river, and the amazing Waddell Memorial Presbyterian on the Orange Side, both built in 1874. In a fascinating collection of buildings for such a small village, there also are Italianate buildings and Victorian farmhouses. At the old Village Depot you will find Retreat Farm Natural Meats and Vegetables, featuring organic produce, locally produced foods, and a potter-in-residence. From Culpeper, south on Route 522 to Route 615.

Follow Route 15 south out of Culpeper. It's not long before the view opens on both sides and Cedar Mountain comes into view. Five and a half miles south of town, see signs for Cedar Mountain Battlefield and turn right onto Route 691.

Cedar Mountain Battlefield. The Civil War Preservation Trust has purchased the primary acreage of this battlefield and begun to interpret the action. It is a battle that nearly ended in a Northern rout of a much larger Southern force. Stonewall Jackson, true to his name, rode into the line of fire waving his sword to rally his troops. As reinforcements came, Southern troops cleared the field. There is a one-mile interpretive trail describing the various phases of battle. You can also just stand in the field and admire the captivating view of Cedar Mountain. This ranks among the most scenic of battlefields. www.civilwar.org/historyclassroom/hc_cedarmountainhist.htm.

Photo: Mike DeHart

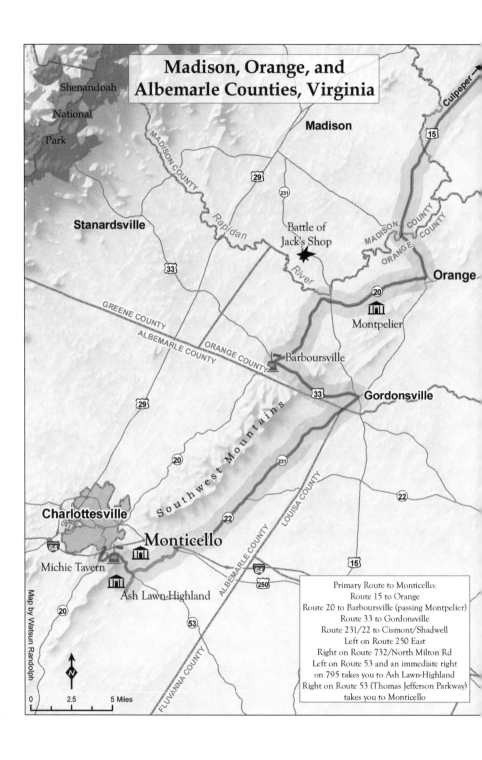

Madison, Orange, and Albemarle Counties, Virginia

Shenandoah

National

Park

Madison

MADISON COUNTY

Culpeper

15

29

231

Stanardsville

Rapidan

Battle of
Jack's Shop

MADISON COUNTY

ORANGE COUNTY

Orange

33

River

20

GREENE COUNTY

Montpelier

ALBEMARLE COUNTY

ORANGE COUNTY

29

Barboursville

33

Gordonsville

Southwest Mountains

20

231

22

22

LOUISA COUNTY

Charlottesville

64

Monticello

Michie Tavern

ALBEMARLE COUNTY

15

64

Ash Lawn-Highland

250

20

53

FLUVANNA COUNTY

N

Map by Watsun Randolph

0   2.5   5 Miles

Primary Route to Monticello:
Route 15 to Orange
Route 20 to Barboursville (passing Montpelier)
Route 33 to Gordonsville
Route 231/22 to Cismont/Shadwell
Left on Route 250 East
Right on Route 732/North Milton Rd
Left on Route 53 and an immediate right
on 795 takes you to Ash Lawn-Highland
Right on Route 53 (Thomas Jefferson Parkway)
takes you to Monticello

Chapter 4

The Journey Through
Madison, Orange, and Albemarle Counties, Virginia

Distance: 39 MILES

HIGHLIGHTS ALONG THE JOURNEY THROUGH HALLOWED GROUND

Miles	Site
0	CULPEPER/MADISON COUNTY LINE
8	ORANGE
12	MONTPELIER
20	BARBOURSVILLE
32	GORDONSVILLE
52	ASH LAWN–HIGHLAND
54	MONTICELLO
56	CHARLOTTESVILLE

Cross Crooked Run and enter Madison County, chartered in 1792 and named for the future president's family who owned considerable lands along the Rapidan River.

Over the next forty-two miles, the road passes the homes and birthplaces of four presidents, several U.S. senators and Virginia governors, delegates to the constitutional conventions of Virginia

Monticello. Photo: CMW

and the United States, and other notable figures. Three of the first five U.S. presidents—Jefferson, Madison, and Monroe—could sometimes be seen talking together at the Charlottesville courthouse. And only thirty miles west of Charlottesville is the birthplace of President Woodrow Wilson. Is there something in the water here?

Maybe there is magic in these foothills. Whatever their capacity to inspire, the rolling hills and mountains are on display at every turn of the road. At the Rapidan River, enter Orange County—named for William of Orange, not the fruit. But why not the orange itself? In spring, when the grasses are lush and the roadbeds lined with wildflowers, the air is positively sweet as citrus.

At the risk of stereotyping, the people are as friendly as the scenery. Even out on the main road in the countryside, traffic sometimes comes to a stop so you can cross back to your car after reading a roadside historical marker. Disarmed by the politeness, you give an animated wave. The nod of the driver's baseball cap to acknowledge your thank-you is almost imperceptible—measurable only by those devices astronomers use to detect the magnetic effect of one distant galaxy on another, an Orange County roadside "you're welcome."

With 28,000 residents, it is among the most rural counties along the Journey. Mile after mile of scenic roads are inviting to bicyclists and motorists. It is perhaps best known as the birthplace of James Madison; it's also the birthplace of Zachary Taylor, twelfth president. Orange County is today a top grape-and-wine-producing county in Virginia, home of two of the largest vineyards in the state and many smaller growers who supply them.

On to Albemarle. Among the county's first settlers were Abraham Lewis and Nicholas Meriwether. In 1735, Lewis obtained eight hundred acres, which now includes the University of Virginia grounds, while Meriwether secured more than a thousand acres in what would become eastern Charlottesville. A generation later Lucy Meriwether married William Lewis. Their son Meriwether Lewis rose to the rank of captain in the army, became Thomas Jefferson's private secretary, and an eponymous leader in the Lewis and Clark

Expedition. President Jefferson, who conceived the idea of the expedition, officially dubbed it the Voyage of Discovery. A marker identifies the site of Lewis's birth on Route 250 west of Charlottesville.

Albemarle was the home of Thomas Jefferson, a person whose influence on American democracy is taught to every school kid. Two of his masterwork designs—Monticello and the University of Virginia complex, which includes the Rotunda, the Lawn, and Pavilions—are together designated World Heritage Sites; there are only twenty such sites in the United States.

Another of his great influences is visible throughout Albemarle and Orange counties, with more evidence being planted each year. Vineyards, that is. Although he was never successful as a vintner, his research, investment, and promotion of winemaking in America, and in Virginia especially, are today considered the roots of America's wine revolution. Memorials come in many forms. There are monuments, museums, and battlefields, to be sure. Still, at the turn of the next century, possibly the greatest memorial to Jefferson would be a still rural landscape along this road, with hill after hill planted in vineyards.

Madison County

Route 15 roughly follows the same course taken in 1716 by Alexander Spotswood and his exploring party, known as the Knights of the Golden Horseshoe. It was an eighteenth-century version of a "media familiarization tour," through which Spotswood wanted to show potential speculators the opportunities of this region and, more importantly, the Shenandoah Valley. They are said to have camped in Madison on the night of August 31. Modern travelers will agree it's a mighty scenic route, with two-centuries-old grand plantation homes overlooking the valley.

One you will pass is the Inn at Meander Plantation. This 1776 plantation house is now a country inn with a Robinson River prospect and views of the Blue Ridge.

A little further, on the right, look for a wayside sign marking the entrance to Woodberry School. The school was founded in 1889 by Robert Stringfellow Walker, a captain in Mosby's Rangers. It was established on land formerly owned by William Madison, brother of the fourth U.S. president and seven-term delegate in the Virginia House. Madison's home, known as The Residence, was built in 1793 and is listed on the National Register of Historic Places. Although the school is not open to the public daily, there are events throughout the year that enable the public to see the grounds.

Beyond the intersection with Route 230 and just before crossing the Rapidan River (formerly the Rapid Ann) into Orange County, is a sign for Madison Mills. The first drive on the right is Greenway, also known as Prospect Hill. This was the home of Francis Madison, also a brother of the president. Built circa 1780 and listed on the National Register of Historic Places, the house is still occupied by descendents of Francis Madison's extended family (it's not open to the public).

Crossing the river into Orange County ends the Journey's brief passage through Madison County. For information on sites in Madison County, see Lodging and Exploring the Countryside in Madison County. See also Create Your Own Journey.

Town of Orange

For all its history, the town of Orange has a down home modesty about it. Maybe that's why town boosters often proclaim Orange's proximity to other places—as in "we're so close to . . ." And while this is true, Orange has an appeal all its own.

Orange attracts artists as residents and summer folk. There are two galleries in town, with reports of other gallery owners eyeing the place like Civil War advance men scouting a bivouac site. There is also a sense of transformation underway, as one by one old buildings take on new purpose. Two new cafes opened in early 2006 alone.

Orange is a terrific walking town for people who enjoy architecture, in part due to the variety. As a result of a terrible fire in 1908, which destroyed Railroad Avenue and the north side of East Main Street, one entire block is of early twentieth-century vintage. Visually, this block is like a separate town. West Main, on the other hand, has the look of a slower evolution, beginning in the 1830s and continuing into the 1930s.

Taylor Park, a pocket garden on West Main, is dedicated to the great grandparents of Presidents Madison and Taylor. On a hot Virginia afternoon, the fountain's spray seems to lower the temperature by degrees, making it just the place for kicking back with a book.

📖 Tours

Downtown Orange Commercial Historic District. There are thirty-nine stops along this self-guided walking tour. A brochure produced by the Orange Downtown Alliance is available at the train station visitor center, 122 E. Main St. Stops include St. Thomas Episcopal Church, a Roman Revival building dating to 1833; it is the church where Robert E. Lee worshiped while in the area. The Sparks Building and Holladay House, both built in 1830, are the two oldest structures in town. Sparks Bistro now operates in the old butchery. Holladay House has been a B&B since 1989. While at the visitor center, pick up a copy of *It Happened in Orange*, a brochure full of Orange in history.

Tourguide, Ltd., Orange County Heritage Tours. Because Orange County was so fiercely contested during the Civil War, the war often gets top billing on the history marquee. But considering the Madisons arrived at Montpelier in 1723, there is much more to the story of Orange. Frank S. Walker, Jr., lead guide for the group, has crafted tours based on a range of heritage themes. One covers only the Madison family estates, for example. Custom itineraries available—yes, including big battles of the Civil War. (540) 672-9414.

Orange Historic District. Photo: Steven L. Spring

James Madison's Montpelier.
Photo: Courtesy of The Montpelier Foundation

🏛 HISTORICAL SITES AND HERITAGE MUSEUMS

James Madison's Montpelier

The estate at Montpelier was in the Madison family from 1723 to 1844, and in the duPont family from 1900 until 1983. The duPont ownership is significant because it was Marion duPont Scott who bequeathed the fourth president's home to the National Trust for Historic Preservation. Her will specifies a desire for the home to be restored "in such a manner as to conform as nearly as possible with the architectural pattern which existed when said property was owned and occupied by President Madison."

Madison is called the Father of the Constitution. It was an honor he was reluctant to embrace, given his modesty and regard for his fellow delegates to the Constitutional Convention of 1787.

The Madison plan put forth the idea of a nation of states, rather than the confederation of independent nation-states formed through the Revolution. In fact, the Constitutional Convention was called to fix some problems in the Articles of Confederation—not necessarily to throw them out.

Some delegates advocated a more dominant central government, while others sought only to tweak the Articles of Confederation. One plan called for senators to be chosen for life by state legislators; the president would then be chosen by the Senate! The meeting was so secret that its records were ordered sealed until sixty years after the last participant had died.

It was Madison's plan and his ability to articulate a vision for a working government that moved the Constitution to approval by delegates, then the Congress, then the states themselves. At the time, he was thirty-six years old.

Montpelier offers an extraordinary window on America from the Piedmont's frontier days through the founding of the nation to the early Antebellum period—Abraham Lincoln was elected only sixteen years after Dolley Madison sold the plantation. In addition to the "home tour," there are exhibits on plantation life and the lives of the enslaved community at Montpelier. Exhibits interpreting the duPont years are also planned—and the annual Montpelier Hunt Races, a tradition begun in 1924, continues. Open daily. Four miles south of Orange on Route 20 (11407 Constitution Highway); (540) 672-2728; www.Montpelier.org.

Ballard-Marshall House

The Ballard-Marshall House was built in 1832 for Garland Ballard, a local merchant. The craftsmanship and details indicate a probable connection with craftsmen once employed by Thomas Jefferson. In 1882 it became the home of Fielding Lewis Marshall, the local superintendent of public education and grandson of Chief Justice John Marshall. Like most private residences on the historic walking tour, the home is not open to the public, but is a worthy stop on the tour. 138 E. Main Street.

Madison's Liberty Temple, a favorite retreat at Montpelier.
Photo: Steven L. Spring

James Madison Museum

The museum features personal belongings of James Madison, including furniture, books, and letters. It also presents the rural heritage of Orange County throughout its history, from farm techniques to agricultural technology. Unless you go, you won't understand the context of a 1924 Model T Ford in a museum named for Madison. Admission is charged, but it's a bargain. If you find yourself within twenty-five miles of Orange, you have to go. Open Monday through Friday year round; Saturdays and Sundays, March through December. 129 Caroline St.; (540) 672-1776; www.jamesmadisonmus.org.

Orange County Courthouse

The Italianate-style building, with its central tower and overhanging eaves, will stop you in your tracks. It's that impressive. If you hear car horns, it's because a motorist approaching from the south is stopped at the traffic light to stare at the courthouse and has not noticed the light change. This is the town's third courthouse, built in 1859. It's at the junction of N. Main St. and Madison Rd.; (540) 672-3313.

Orange County Courthouse. Photo: Steven L. Spring

Orange Historical Society

When Orange County was formed in 1734, it was the largest county in Virginia. In fact, it included all of what are now the states of Kentucky, Illinois, Ohio, Indiana, and parts of others—all territory claimed by Virginia (and some of it claimed by other states, as well). In addition to its services as a research library, the society sells books on local history and historical maps, and offers programs open to the public. Stop in to see what's on the calendar. 130 Caroline St.; (540) 672-5366.

Orange Railway Station

After the fire of 1908 destroyed the old depot, this Colonial Revival station, complete with gable roof and wrap-around overhang, was built to serve the Orange and Alexandria line. Today it houses the visitor center; 122 E. Main St.

Wilderness Battlefield

May 1864 was the first time General U.S. Grant, newly appointed commander of all Federal armies, faced off against Confederate General Robert E. Lee. Two days of ruthless, often hand-to-hand fighting in a tangle of thicket and underbrush, resulted in 25,000 casualties. There is no visitor center at Wilderness, but there is an exhibit shelter on Route 20. In summer, the historians at the shelter answer questions and offer short programs (weekends only in spring and autumn). In winter months, you can learn about Wilderness from staff and docents in the Fredericksburg and Chancellorsville visitor centers. Route 20, Wilderness, Va.

☕ EATING OUT, HANGING OUT

Lunch and Casual Fare

Dave's Deli and Café. Located in the historic Levy Building at the corner of Main and Railroad Ave., Dave's is open for breakfast until 8 p.m., Monday through Saturday. For lunch, there are subs, sandwiches, homemade soups and deli salads, and a few entrees. You can get picnic fixings to go from the deli case. 118 E. Main St.; (540) 672-5569.

El Vaquero West. The food is fresh and the service is excellent. Open daily. 215 Madison Rd.; (540) 672-3880.

Happy Garden Chinese Restaurant. Walkable from in-town B&Bs and open until 10 p.m. Also open Sundays. 130 E. Main St.; (540) 672-1044.

Mario's Pizza and Pasta Buffet. The name says it; a fitting finish to a day spent hiking or cycling. 269 Madison Rd.; (540) 672-3344.

Not The Same Old Grind and Orange Roasters. Coffees from twenty countries roasted and blended on site, complemented by a café serving breakfast and lunch—with an emphasis on healthy eating. 130 E. Church St.; www.orange roasters.com. (540) 672-3143

Silk Mill Grille. Located in the historic Silk Mill Building, once the busiest silk mill in the U.S., where parachutes were churned out during World War II; the fare is casual American. 101 Woodmark St.; (540) 672-4010.

Sparks Bistro. In one of two Orange structures constructed in 1830, the building is the oldest one in town by a few months—but the food is always fresh. Salads and sandwiches. For a taste of Virginia, try the Rapidan, which features honey-glazed ham and onions. Open until 3 p.m. 124 E. Main St.; (540) 672-0060.

Dining

Inn at Meander Plantation. A few miles north of Orange on Route 15 in Madison County, the inn features an elegant five-course dinner, with one seating at 7 p.m. Reservations required; open Thursday through Saturday. See Lodging for more information. 2333 N. James Madison Hwy., Locust Dale. (540) 672-4912; www.meander.net.

Willow Grove Inn. Famous for its lodging as well as its food, the inn was built in the late eighteenth century and expanded in 1848; it is on the National Register of Historic Places. Serving dinner Wednesday through Saturday from 6 p.m., and brunch on Sundays beginning at 11 p.m. Call for reservations. One mile north of town on Route 15 at 14079 Plantation Way; (540) 672-5982; www.willowgroveinn.com.

Willow Grove Inn and grounds. Photo: Steven L. Spring

✠ DISTINCTIVE SHOPS AND STOPS

The Art Center in Orange. The gallery's exhibits feature painting and sculpture from the region and beyond; the gallery store is a Virginia-made smorgasbord selling pottery, ceramics, music, books, and other arts and items by Virginia artists and artisans. 129 E. Main St.; www.orangeartcenter.org.

A Classic Touch Consigned Furniture. You never know what will be on the floor, but it's always worth a look. Tuesday through Saturday. 109 E. Main St.

Hare Hill. This shop features antique china and glassware, with an extensive selection of Blue Willow in its many, many forms. 112 E. Main St.

J.S. Mosby Antiques and Artifacts. Specializing in Civil War relics, books, and memorabilia, plus World Wars I and II, and other general military memorabilia. Open Wednesday through Saturday. 125 E. Main St; www.jsmosby.com.

Library Used Book Store. This adjunct to the Orange Public Library has thousands of hardcover and paperbacks books of all genres. 220 N. Fifth St.

Melrose Antiques. Several rooms of furnishings, rugs, and decorative arts, including decoys and other wildlife art. 101 E. Main St.

Taylor Park. This is a gem of a park with a fountain and gravel garden path. If you're grabbing lunch to go, this is the place to take it. Nice for an afternoon cuppa, too. The park plays host to a summer concert series and farmers market. On West Main St.

⌑ LODGING

In Orange

Greenock House Inn. The expansive grounds, gardens, and porches offer a feeling of being out in the foothills, but this nineteenth-century home is on the edge of town. The food is the primary attraction here; you can order bistro suppers served in your room or prix fixe for several guests. 249 Caroline St.; (540) 672-3625; www.greenockhouse.com.

Holladay House. Main Street's only B&B was built in 1830 and is one of the two oldest buildings in Orange. Subsequent additions have created a spacious manor offering guests plenty of privacy. The inn's Victorian Suite overlooks Main Street; rooms feature fireplaces and double Jacuzzi baths. 155 W. Main St.; (540) 672-4893; www.holladayhouse bandb.com.

Inn on Poplar Hill. Within town limits, yet with twenty-eight acres to wander. Ten acres are in wildflowers, encircled by a mowed path. The elegant home was built in the 1890s by Thomas Jefferson's great-granddaughter. 278 Caroline St.; (540) 672-6840; www.innonpoplarhill.com.

Mayhurst Inn. Colonel John Willis was a great-grandnephew of James Madison. Mayhurst Plantation consisted of 2,500 acres. Constructed in 1858, the home is an Italianate wonder of interior design. On the estate's thirty-seven acres you will still find the smokehouse, summer kitchen, patio, and gardens. And there is a lovely pond. The house is listed on the National Register. Just south of town at 12460 Mayhurst Lane; (540) 672-5597; www.mayhurstinn.com.

Inn at Meander Plantation

In the Country

Inn at Meander Plantation. In Madison County along Route 15. This is spot-on elegance in a historic plantation house surrounded by views and solitude. Dinner is available to guests each night and to the public Thursday through Saturday. 2333 N. James Madison Hwy., Locust Dale. (540) 672-4912; (800) 385-4936; www.meander.net.

Sleepy Hollow Farm. A quiet country retreat in a private hollow, this B&B has a pond with a dock and gazebo for enjoying late afternoons. The inn is welcoming to pets, too. 16280 Blue Ridge Turnpike, Gordonsville. (540) 832-5555; www.sleepyhollowfarmbnb.com.

Willow Grove Inn. People find it hard to describe this grand, historic inn, its food and hospitality without resorting to superlatives. Just north of town on Route 15 at 14079 Plantation Way; (540) 672-5982; www.willowgroveinn.com.

⚲ EXPLORING THE COUNTRYSIDE

Wineries

Barboursville Vineyards. One of Virginia's largest vineyards, on the estate of Governor James Barbour (see Barbours-ville). Winery Rd., Barboursville; (540) 832-3824; www.barbours villewine.com.

Burnley Vineyards. One of the oldest vineyards in the region, this small family vineyard also is the "value vineyard" of the region, with most wines priced right around $10. At 4500 Winery Lane, Barboursville; (540) 832-2828; www.burnleywines.com.

Horton Vineyards. Perhaps Virginia's most widely distributed labels and most visited vineyards. Best known for reviving viognier varietals in Virginia. 6399 Spotswood Trail (Route 33), Gordonsville; (540) 832-7440.

Outdoor Recreation

Hiking Trails along Skyline Drive. Just a short drive west is Skyline Drive and Shenandoah National Park. Take a scenic drive, hike, have a picnic, or take a family ride on horseback (no experience required). If you're up for a hike, walk a mile down into Hoover Camp, the summer retreat built by President Hoover, now a National Landmark. In summer, volunteers can give you a tour of the outside of the buildings. www.nps.gov/shen

Photo: CMW

Old Rag Mountain. Take a hike up "Old Raggedy" in Shenandoah National Park. Accessible from Route 231 north of Madison, the mountain boasts some of the best views in the Blue Ridge. If you're an experienced hiker, or traveling with one, you can take a full-moon hike up the mountain (take a flashlight and watch out for snakes!).

Town of Madison. A scenic one-street town in Madison County, Madison has a handsome courthouse listed on the Virginia Historic Register and a museum in the Madison Arcade, which was built in 1790 as is listed on the National Register of Historic Places. Hebron Lutheran Church, built in 1740, is said to be the oldest Lutheran church in continuous use in the United States. The 1834 Piedmont Episcopal Church was remodeled in the 1920s using walnut paneling donated by First Lady Hoover. At the north end of town is the **Madison Inn Restaurant**, located in a historic building and serving nouvelle American.

Hiking couple on Old Rag Mountain. Photo: CMW

Motoring south on Route 15 from Orange, The Journey Through Hallowed Ground picks up Virginia Route 20 en route to Charlottesville. The pastoral country around you is the Madison-Barboursville Historic District, a forty-square mile rural landscape recognized for its heritage and beauty. For the next eight miles the view is of rolling farmland punctuated every mile or so by a magnificent plantation home.

At the junction with Route 20 is **Old Somerset**. The charming chapel is **Somerset Christian Church**. Built circa 1857, its Italianate bracketed cornice and porch are a departure from the Gothic and Greek Revival styles of most nineteenth-century Virginia country churches. The structure is virtually unaltered from its original appearance; the interior retains its original furnishings, including its pews. From here, look south, back toward **Gordonsville**, for an open view of **Somerset House**, home of Thomas Macon and Sarah Catlett Madison Macon, sister of President Madison.

The Journey route travels south along Route 231 from here, but first takes an interlude to Barboursville. Traveling south on Route 20, pass through the hamlet of Tibbstown, then cross Route 33 on a double dogleg left into Barboursville and Barboursville Plantation.

Barboursville

A crossroad town now, Barboursville grew up around the plantation home of James Barbour, Virginia governor, 1812-14. He also served as U.S. senator from Virginia (1815-25) and secretary of war (1825-28). His home was designed by close friend Thomas Jefferson, completed in 1822. That Jefferson would design a home for his friend is not surprising, but that he somehow managed to fit the task into his schedule while also developing plans for the University of Virginia (and his perpetual Monticello projects) is testament to Jefferson's voracious appetite for work. By all accounts, it was a celebrated structure and Jeffersonian masterpiece. It was destroyed by fire on Christmas Day, 1884, but even the ruins are a thing of beauty. They are open to the public. The ruins are on the grounds of **Barboursville Vineyards**, a one-thousand-acre estate featuring an elegant inn and the **Paladio Restaurant**.

Governor Barbour Street is the home of **Nichols Galleries**, two art galleries owned by Frederick and Beth Nichols. At **Nichols Gallery Annex**, where the entire historic house is given over to gallery space, Beth shows the work of noted artists and new artists she promotes. A few doors down is **Frederick Nichols Studio**, the artist's gallery and printmaking shop. Nichols' unique use of color in landscape painting has won him decades of admirers. At heart, he's just a hiker with a colorful imagination who paints. You'll see his paintings in big city galleries, but you'll find Nichols in the old general store that is studio and home. Nichols' other art form is the silk screen, some of which involve forty or more color passes. Both Frederick and Beth offer occasional demonstrations in silk screen printmaking. Gallery hours: Thursday through Sunday, 11 to 5. (540) 832-3565; www.frednichols.com.

Retrace your path north on Route 20 five miles to Old Somerset and turn right on Route 231, the Blue Ridge Turnpike. Drive approximately seven miles to the junction with Route 33; turn right. At the traffic circle, go straight on Route 15 to enter Gordonsville on Main Street.

Gordonsville

The town was named for Nathaniel Gordon, a late eighteenth-century innkeeper here, whose tavern was frequented by such prominent statesmen as Thomas Jefferson and Major General the Marquis de Lafayette

The Civil War Museum at the Exchange Hotel, the anchor of the Gordonsville's historic district and the town's main attraction, is on the National Register of Historic Places. Its focus is the Civil War, but it also interprets a fascinating part of American history—rural railroad hotels. Before air conditioning and cars and shopping malls, people left the city on rails for cool country breezes on a hotel porch. Before the Civil War, the Exchange was a well-appointed, comfortable hotel which served passengers of two railroads. It became the Gordonsville Receiving Hospital, treating more than seventy thousand wounded and sick soldiers from Chancellorsville, Wilderness, and other battles in the area. It was primarily a Confederate hospital but treated Union soldiers, as well. Built in 1860, the building is listed on the National Register of Historic Places and is owned by Historic Gordonsville, which operates the museum. Open until 4 p.m. (closed Wednesdays), mid-March through mid-December. 400 S. Main St.; Gordonsville; (540) 832-2944; www.hgiexchange.org.

On Main Street, a shop called **Homespun** features folk art, imported gifts, and antiques. **Country Gardens** sells ornamental lawn and garden objects, and **Old Somerset Gallery** sells fine furnishings and art. There are a couple of casual eateries (go to **Mama's** at 205 N. Main Street for great chili and **601 Deli** for burgers).

For full service dining, there are two worthy choices. **Restaurant Pomme** has classic old world French cuisine (by a Frenchman, no less) in a warm, understated ambiance. It's a good stop for lunch after a visit to the Exchange Hotel or dinner after touring the wineries. Reservations recommended. Tuesday through Saturday, noon to 2:30 p.m. and 6 p.m. to 8:30 p.m.; Sunday brunch, noon to 2:30 p.m. 115 S. Main St., Gordonsville, Va. (540) 832-0130. **Tolliver House,** located on North Main Street, features nicely turned American fare in a charming restored Victorian house—dine outside on the porch. Lunch and dinner, Wednesday through Sunday. (540) 832-0000.

Return to the traffic circle and continue to follow 231South/ Gordonsville Road. This is a beautiful drive any time of year. In about 10 miles, in the village of **Cismont**, Route 231 becomes Route 22. Continue straight onto Route 22/Louisa Road.

Reach Thomas Jefferson's birthplace, **Shadwell**, in about six miles. A wayside sign marks the location.

At Shadwell make a hard left onto Route 250 East. Make an immediate right at the stop light onto Route 729/North Milton Road. Cross over the Rivanna River and make a right onto Route 732/Milton Road. Follow Milton Road to the intersection of Route 53 (**Brix Marketplace** is at this intersection).

Turn left, then immediately right onto Route 795, James Monroe Parkway. Ash Lawn–Highland, the home of James Monroe, is a half mile further on the right.

James Monroe's Ash Lawn–Highland

Ash Lawn-Highland

James Monroe was fifth President of the United States, U.S. Senator and Governor of Virginia. He and his wife Elizabeth purchased a thousand acres near Monticello in 1793. Monroe named it Highland. Although they hoped to move there immediately, in 1794 Monroe was appointed Minister Plenipotentiary to France by

Cooking demonstration at James Monroe's Ash Lawn-Highland.
Photo: Steven L. Spring

President Washington. The house Monroe referred to as his "cabin-castle" was completed upon his return in 1797, but it would be two more years before the family moved in and made it home.

Monroe is a president who deserves our getting to know, and Highland is a wonderful place to start. He served and was wounded in Washington's army as they crossed the Delaware River at Trenton. He traveled to Paris for Jefferson with the intention of buying New Orleans, and returned with the entire Louisiana Territory. As president, Monroe acquired Florida and articulated the nation's first foreign policy, now known as the Monroe Doctrine. By the time he became President, he had served as Minster to France, England, and Spain for Presidents Washington and Jefferson; and Secretary of State and War for President Madison.

He and his family loved Highland. Throughout his two term presidency, he spoke of building a larger house at Highland and retiring there to farm and be close to Jefferson and James Madison. Unfortunately, after his more than fifty years of public service—a hardship in an era in which officials financed their own travel and expenses—he found himself terribly in debt. He sold Highland and retired to his Loudoun County property, Oak Hill.

A later owner changed the name of the property to Ash Lawn. Eventually, the property was bequeathed to the College of William and Mary, Monroe's alma mater. Now the home is known as Ash Lawn-Highland. The College began its ongoing program of research, restoration, and interpretation at Ash Lawn-Highland in 1975.

Monroe's cabin-castle is a warm place to visit for its human scale and the family stories behind the art and objects displayed, including a large collection of original Monroe furnishings.. You can wander the intimate gardens and outbuildings and visit the farm animals. There are farm-craft demonstrations and children's games too. You can even get married or host events there. In summer, there are opera and chamber music performances in the garden—plus the occasional Broadway revue. Begun in 1978, the annual opera festival now includes six to eight weeks of full-length opera and musical theater productions, lectures, the Music at Twilight program and Summer Saturdays series arts programs. All of this is fitting for a president who enjoyed entertaining and wanted nothing more of his home than for it to be a "place of comfort and hospitality." Open daily, Route 795, 2.5 miles from Monticello. (434) 293-9539, www.ashlawnhighland.org

———

Leaving Ash Lawn–Highland, turn left and retrace a half mile back to Thomas Jefferson Parkway. Turn left and follow this scenic road 1.5 miles to Monticello, on the left.

Monticello

Every time you think you understand the breadth of Thomas Jefferson's influence, Monticello reveals a little more. The world famous house and plantation that surround it served as Jefferson's laboratory for revolutionary landscape, architectural, political, and domestic ideas.

Monticello—Jefferson's mountaintop home—is the autobiographical masterpiece of Thomas Jefferson, designed and redesigned and built and rebuilt for more than forty years. Jefferson

gave form to the nascent United States through his philosophical writings and his service. More literally, he did so through his architectural innovation. Jefferson's plans for Monticello, based upon the architecture of classical antiquity, symbolize the aspirations of the new American republic.

Of the many honors awarded to Monticello, one of the most prestigious and unique honors is its status as a World Heritage Site (in conjunction with the University of Virginia), it is the only private residence on the World Heritage Site list.

The gardens at Monticello were a botanic showpiece, a source of food, and an experimental laboratory of ornamental and useful plants from around the world. Ongoing research has led to new discoveries and new exhibits. The re-creation of orchards, forests, and vineyards tell us even more about Jefferson's advanced thinking on soils, husbandry, and viticulture. Jefferson, for example, was an early adopter of cover crops to "fix nitrogen" into the soil. He was

Thomas Jefferson's Monticello. Photo: Steve L. Spring

also perhaps the first American to espouse healthy soils as essential to both plant nutrition and to a plant's ability to ward off pests.

Each season of the year brings a different perspective on Monticello and on Jefferson—so everyone must visit at least four times! During the three warm seasons, there are the gardens and orchards. There are children skipping along paths and laughing from one end of Monticello's "all weather passage" to the other. Jefferson would be pleased to see these visiting kids enjoying the day; he would delight in watching a parent identify a flower or bird to a young child. In his later years, he had a house full of grandchildren and loved it. His daughter Martha, her husband, and twelve children lived at Monticello.

Monticello also reveals an American culture with which many of us are unfamiliar. Early Americans, for example, did not really eat fruit—they drank it. Apples were for cider and peaches were for brandy. Jefferson actually ate the stuff. He had an orchard for beverage fruits and one for fruits and nuts to eat. He served beer or cider with supper every day; wine was an after dinner drink.

The Monticello plantation of 5,000 acres was a center of agriculture and industry, and was home not only to the Jefferson family, but to workers, black and white, enslaved and free. Monticello offers a rare thorough picture of life on a nineteenth-century Southern plantation. It contrasts the lives of those inside the mansion with the workers who served the plantation, both enslaved and free. As research reveals more about Monticello's enslaved community, these discoveries are presented alongside other facts about Jefferson.

Garden Tours of Jefferson's restored flower and vegetable gardens, grove, and orchards are available April 1-October 31. Tours, which last about 45 minutes, begin on the West Lawn at 9:15, 10:15, 11:15, 12:15, 1:15, 2:15, 3:15, and 4:15 daily. Tickets are included in the price of admission.

Plantation Tours are also available April 1-October 31. These guided tours, included in the price of admission, focus on African-American life at Monticello.

Monticello is open daily, except Christmas Day. To make advance reservations, www. monticello.org

Kitchen gardens and view at Monticello. Photo: Steven L. Spring

After visiting the house and Plantations, why not take a tour of Montalto, Jefferson's High Mountain. The panoramas from Montalto afford visitors sweeping panoramas not only of the house and plantation, but also of Charlottesville, the Blue Ridge, the Southwest Moutains Rural Historic District (including Jefferson's Birthplace at Shadwell, located on Route 250 East). Monalto tours are offered seasonally May1-October 31 at 1 p.m. and 3 p.m..

Departing Monticello, turn left and descend Mt. Alto on Route 53. While you're still in a Jefferson frame of mind, you can stop at a Colonial tavern.

Michie Tavern (pronounced "Mickey") is more than a single tavern. Historic structures from other locations have been re-constructed here to serve as commercial operations, with one selling colonial clothing and gifts and another serving as a mercantile shop. The tavern offers a Southern-style buffet, served in the setting of an "ordinary." It's a sentimental, but altogether engaging place—the fried chicken is good too. Adjacent to the tavern is the museum,

The cemetery at Monticello. Photo: Steven L. Spring

a 1784 building presenting eighteenth-century tavern life. If you purchase a Presidential Pass, you get a discount on the combined entrance to Monticello, Ash Lawn-Highland, and Michie Tavern. 683 Thomas Jefferson Parkway; (434) 977-1234; www.michie tavern.com.

———

Turn left from Michie Tavern. At the intersection with Route 20, turn right toward Charlottesville. The visitor center on the left has a terrific exhibit on the life and times of Thomas Jefferson.

Monticello concludes the southbound heritage tour of the Journey Through Hallowed Ground that begins in Gettysburg, Pennsylvania. It is a proper finish to the Journey, but by no means the end of your travels through this unique landscape. The lovely city of Charlottesville, home of Thomas Jefferson's University of Virginia, is just a couple of miles from the bottom of the hill.

Charlottesville

When the Virginia legislature and Governor Thomas Jefferson fled Virginia's capital to evade British troops in 1781, they came to Charlottesville. At the time, the town consisted of a courthouse, tavern, and little more than a dozen homes and businesses. Even the first rendition of Jefferson's Monticello, on a mountain above the town, was barely finished. Decades later, as Jefferson founded the University of Virginia, the town was still no more than a rural village.

As you explore these parts, you might imagine what Jefferson would think of today's Charlottesville. The man who idealized the agrarian would agree this small city upholds some of his key ideals. It is rich in the arts and music, lively in civic engagement, and has a highly educated populace. One thing is for sure: Jefferson would love The Mall, the eight-block, car-free commercial area of East Main Street. He would go for the bookstores, street conversation, and the bustling enterprise of independently owned businesses. It is easy to imagine Jefferson in a C'Ville coffee shop debating public policy or pining over Patty Larkin's performance at the Gravity Lounge.

Charlottesville is big enough to make days of walking its historic streets. It is also small enough to walk from the east end of the downtown to the University of Virginia on the west end of Main. On the University Grounds you will see the celebrated Rotunda, Jefferson's centerpiece of his "academical village." It is considered among the most beautiful buildings in America. If the return walk is too much, you can take the free trolley that travels the route until midnight daily, stopping at roughly one-block intervals.

📖 TOURS

For information on guided walking tours, see Albemarle Charlottesville Historical Society below. For an excellent self-guiding reference, pick up a copy of the *Historic Charlottesville Tour Book*. The book describes ten tours of the city, complete with easy-to-use maps and walking/driving directions between each stop. Available at the Historical Society and at most bookstores in town (even used book stores tend to carry new copies of this informative guide).

🏛 HISTORICAL SITES AND HERITAGE MUSEUMS

Albemarle Charlottesville Historical Society

In addition to exhibits depicting county and regional history, the historical society houses an extensive research library and hosts public programs, including a popular series of guided walks through Charlottesville's historic neighborhoods. A guided walk of the downtown mall area is offered every other Saturday. 200 Second St., NE; (434) 296-1492; www.albemarlehistory.org.

The Corner

This is the compact commercial area across from the UVA campus. According to the Albemarle Historical Society, the name was given by students in the early 1900s for the then-small collection of stores across from campus on University Avenue. Today, the Corner is packed with eateries serving up pizza, sandwiches, and an array of international foods, along with a few boutiques, a pool hall, and the venerable Virginian restaurant, which has been in business since 1923. The buildings of this historic area date primarily from the 1870s to the 1930s. (For a description of other buildings in the neighborhood, pick up a copy of the *Historic Charlottesville Tour Book*.)

Court Square

The Albemarle County Courthouse is the anchor of the historic collection of houses and shops where the town began. The courthouse was first built in 1803 and has the distinction of seeing Thomas Jefferson, James Madison, and James Monroe as regular visitors, sometimes on the same day.

Across the street from the courthouse at 300 Park Street was the former Swan Tavern. Here Governor Jefferson and the Virginia legislature took up session after fleeing Richmond in May 1781. The contingent included future presidents John Tyler and Benjamin Harrison, plus Richard Henry Lee, Patrick Henry, and, representing Kentucky (then part of Virginia), Daniel Boone. Unbeknownst to the Assembly, the British were in hot pursuit. Jack Jouett, son of the Swan's owner, was at a tavern in Louisa County when he saw 250 mounted men en route to Charlottesville. He rode through the night on back roads and horse trails, arriving at dawn to rouse and warn Jefferson and the Assembly. Many consider Jack Jouett the Southern Paul Revere, who foiled the attempt to kidnap Thomas Jefferson. Seven were captured, among them Boone, who was released a day later.

Jackson Park and Lee Park

From Courthouse Square, walk down Jefferson Street to Jackson Park, then two blocks more to Lee Park. Both were created through contributions by a local philanthropist and contain statues of their namesakes on horseback. The Jackson statue, with Little Sorrel seemingly defying gravity, is a renowned sculpture. Both sculptures were completed in the early 1920s. Lee Park is a gem of a green space, with chess tables and shade trees, taking up a full city block.

The University of Virginia Rotunda. Photo: Steven L. Spring

The University of Virginia Rotunda, Lawn, and Pavilions
A World Heritage Site. Completed in 1826 shortly after
Thomas Jefferson's death, the Rotunda is one of Virginia's
most recognized buildings. Designed by Jefferson to be
the center of an "academical village," the Rotunda stands
at the north end of the Lawn, surrounded on the west by
the Pavilions and student rooms along the east. In the
axiom that great institutions deserve great buildings, the
Rotunda and its surrounding are the superlative by which
others are measured. Tours are free and given daily on the
hour at 10 and 11 a.m., and at 2, 3, and 4 p.m. Even without
entering the building, walking the Lawn and examining
the structures from outside is, to borrow a Jefferson phrase,
worthy of the voyage.

☕ EATING OUT, HANGING OUT

In a city regularly ranked at the top of those "great places to
live" lists, you know you can wander down any Charlottesville
commercial street and find interesting shops and places to eat. Before

you go, check out www.charlottesville-dining.com. One of the city's great treats is a late afternoon stroll to peek at menus posted in windows. Here are just a few places in and near the downtown Mall to fit a range of moods and moneys.

Bizou Diner. On the Mall, creative twists on diner and comfort food. Laid back.119 W. Main St. (434) 977-1818

Café Cubana Coffee. On the Mall at 1st Street, good for breakfast and java. (434) 971-8743

Court Square Tavern. At Court Square, below the sidewalk, like a historic "ordinary" should be. More than one hundred beers featured. 500 Court Square # 305. (434) 296-6111

Felini's #9. Southern Italian cuisine featuring seafood and pasta and an inventive array of salads. A block off the Mall at West 2nd and Market streets. (434) 979-4279

Gravity Lounge. Books, music, coffee and food, music performance (Livingston Taylor, Mary Lou Lord, Odetta, to name a few) . . . somehow the Gravity Lounge does it all. 103 S. 1st St.; (434) 977-5590; www.gravity-lounge.com.

l'etoile. French renditions of Virginia cuisine using many local ingredients. A fine bistro lunch located about halfway between the Corner and Mall. 817 W. Main St. (434) 979-7957

La Cucina. A quiet, warm Italian trattoria. A block off the Mall at 214 W. Water St. (434) 295-9050

Mudhouse Coffee. A local chain and nice, comfy place to hang out. 213 W. Main St. (413) 984-6833

Oxo. French cuisine in the classical tradition, with outdoor seating. A block off the Mall at 215 W. Water St. (434) 977-8111

South Street Brewery. Award-winning brews, a princely bar, and good food. 106 South Street; (434) 293-6550.

✤ DISTINCTIVE SHOPS AND STOPS

Art Upstairs. A cooperative gallery featuring original art by its twenty member artists who work in oil, acrylic, watercolor, paper collage, pastel, ink, graphite, and tapestry. 316 E. Main St., inside the Hardware Store; (434) 923-3900.

The Barn Swallow. Artisan pottery and décor objects. Route 250 W; (434) 979-4884.

Kluge-Ruhe. The Aboriginal art collection of the University of Virginia. 400 Worrell Dr. at Peter Jefferson Pl.; (434) 244-0234; www.Virginia.edu/kluge-ruhe.

McGuffey Art Center. A cooperative studio and exhibit space for members and associate artists located in an old public school. 201 Second Street, NW; (434) 295-7973; www.mcg uffeyartcenter.com.

Sage Moon. Original works in a range of media and styles. 420 E. Main St.; (434) 977-9997; www.sagemoongallery.com.

Second Street Gallery. A small contemporary gallery a block off the Mall; 201 2nd St. NW; (434) 977-7284; www.secondstreetgallery.com.

Seven Very Fine Bookstores. Rarely will you find such an eclectic collection of wonderful bookstores offering used, rare, and antiquarian books—perhaps that's to be expected in a city that hosts the annual Virginia Festival of the Book (www.vabook.org).
  ❖ Avocado Pit; 310 E. Market St. (434) 817-0010.
  ❖ Blue Whale Used & Rare Books; 115 W. Main. (434) 296-4646.

❖ Book Cellar; 316 E. Main St., in the Hardware Store. (434) 979-7787.

❖ Daedalus Books; 124 2nd St. NW. (434) 293-7595.

❖ New Dominion Book Shop; 404 Main St. (434) 295-2552.

❖ Oakley's Gently Used Books; 112 W. Main St. (434) 977-3313.

❖ Read it Again Sam; 214 E. Main St. (434) 977-9844.

Thorn Fine Cabinetmakers. Honoring a Piedmont tradition of fine, custom-made furnishings. 218 W. Main St.; (434) 984-0500.

Transient Crafters. An artisans' cooperative featuring handmade crafts and gifts. 118 E. Main St.; (434) 972-9500; www.transientcrafters.com.

Victoria's Handbag Shop. Original handbags of fine fabric, crafted in the studio as you watch. 316 E. Main St., inside the Hardware Store; (434) 981-4743; www.victoriahorner.com.

Vivian's. Jewelry, glass, pottery, artistic clothing and accessories, and wood-crafted artful home objects. 301 E. Main St.; (804) 977-8908.

🛏 LODGING

Monticello Hotel Partners
(www.monticello.org/visit/hotelpartners): The Cavalier Inn, Keswick Hall at Monticello, Boars Head Inn, The Bed and Breakfast Association of Virginia Central Region, Omni Hotel, Double Tree Hotel Charlottesville, Comfort Inn-Monticello, Marriott Residence Inn Charlottesville.

200 South Street Inn. Two downtown historic homes comprise this spacious inn. Despite careful, meticulous restoration to its former grandeur (after a stint as a brothel) it remains cozy and warm. 200 South Street; (434) 979-0200; www.southstreetinn.com.

Clifton. The estate of Thomas Jefferson's son-in-law, Thomas Mann Randolph, Jr., Virginia governor and U.S. senator. Built in the early nineteenth century while the Randolph family lived at Monticello, the home is listed on the National Register of Historic Places and is considered one of the most elegant inns in the region. 1296 Clifton Inn Dr.; (888) 971-1800; www.cliftoninn.net.

Dinsmore House. James Dinsmore was Monticello's master carpenter and the master carpenter for UVA's Pavilions III, V, VIII, fourteen dormitories, and, with John Neilson, the Rotunda. So you can imagine what the house that bears his name is like. Across from the University Grounds. 1211 W. Main St.; (434)974-4663; www.dinsmorehouse.com.

Inn at Court Square. A small B&B in a remarkable historic building, across from the courthouse in a quiet, peaceful setting— the neighborhood where the village of Charlottesville was founded. An elegant lunch is served, too. 410 E. Jefferson St; (434) 295-2800; www.innatcourtsquare.com.

🚗 To Do in Charlottesville

Attend an Outdoor Opera at Ash Lawn–Highland. Even if you're not a regular at the opera, what could be more charming than a performance in the garden of James Monroe's side yard (see Ash Lawn–Highland).

Go Ice-skating at Charlottesville Ice Park. Rent your skates and slide on the ice at the town rink, located on the Mall. 230 W. Main St.; (434) 817-2400.

Ride the Hatten Ferry. There are only two pole-driven ferries left in America—this is one of them. A few miles outside Scottsville on Route 625. For further information, call the Albemarle Charlottesville Historical Society at (434) 296-1492.

See the Blue Ridge from a Hot Air Balloon. Get 360-degree views of the Piedmont and Blue Ridge high above the hills. Monticello Country Ballooning; (434) 996-9008; www.virginiaballoon.com.

Virginia Discovery Museum. Located at the east end of the Mall, this is a fine kids science center.

 Exploring the Countryside

Wineries

There are more than twenty wineries in the area, together making up the Monticello Wine Trail (www.monticellowinetrail.org). Here are a few notable ones in and near Charlottesville.

Jefferson Vineyards. Located on the land where Jefferson and Felippo Massei established vineyards. The current vineyard was planted in 1981. The winery is adjacent to Monticello, offering outstanding views and highly regarded wines. 1353 Thomas Jefferson Parkway; (800) 272-3042; www.jefferson vineyards.com.

King Family Vineyards. One of Albemarle's craft wineries, located fifteen minutes west of Charlottesville in the mountains. J6550 Roseland Farm, Crozet, Va.; (434) 823-7800; www.kingfamilyvineyards.com.

The scenic Rivanna River. Photo: Steven L. Spring

Oakencroft Vineyard & Winery. The oldest winery in Albemarle County is located in a picturesque setting by a lake. 1486 Oakencroft Lane; (434) 296-4188; www.oakencroft.com.

Outdoor Recreation

You can find solitude and quiet hikes in and around Charlottesville. The Rivanna Trails system encircles the entire city following the banks of three waterways.
http://avenue.org/rivanna.

Kemper Park to Monticello. You can hike a 2.2-mile trail from the base of Route 53 to the grounds of Monticello. At Kemper Park, enjoy the arboretum of native trees and a two-acre pond.

Ragged Mountain Natural Area. Hike the hills loved by Edgar Allan Poe when he was a UVA student at this 980-acre preserve; four miles of trails. On Route 702 (Reservoir Rd.) west of town.

Shenandoah National Park. The southern end of Skyline Drive is off Interstate 64 at the top of the ridge. At the entrance booth, pick up a map and get some information about nearby trails that match your abilities. Take a drive on the Drive.

Small Towns

Fluvanna Courthouse Historic District. You could zoom through the small town of Palmyra on Route 15 without taking note of its historic courthouse district—don't! The Greek Doric courthouse, completed in 1831, is one of the few antebellum courthouses in Virginia in its original form. Adjacent to the courthouse is the Old Stone Jail Museum, featuring local artifacts and historical documents. The courthouse district is a remarkable collection of buildings, one which famed architectural historian Talbot Hamlin deemed the Acropolis of Palmyra. The courthouse, still in use, is open during business hours. Tours are available from the Fluvanna County Historical Society, located in the Old Jail Museum. The museum is open weekends, 1 to 5 on Saturdays and 2:00 to 5 on Sundays, from late-May to late-October. Special tours or group tours are available by appointment: (804) 589-3704. Tours are available in German, Italian, and French, as well as English.

The Road to Monticello. Photo: Steven L. Spring

——— *Chapter* 5 ———

Create Your Own Journey: Scenic Drives to Heritage Sites and Small Towns

There is more to see along The Journey Through Hallowed Ground than can be seen from its main route. After all, the Journey recognizes the landscape through which the route passes. These scenic drives take you into the countryside, where you will encounter breathtaking vistas, out-of-the-way stops and shops, and charming small towns.

Many of the heritage sites described in these scenic drives are also covered in the county-by-county chapters. They're collected here to provided a thematic or scenic connection. For example, this chapter contains an African American Heritage itinerary. The description of James Madison's Montpelier in that itinerary focuses on the African American exhibits and programs at Montpelier. By and large, the descriptions in the county-by-county chapters are fuller, describing the breadth of the programs and exhibits at the sties.

For sites that are described in the county-by-county chapters, you will find contact information there. Contact information is provided in this section only for new entries and only as necessary.

1. A Presidential Journey

Highlights: A visit to sites linked to U.S. presidents: their homes, retreats, and places important to their presidencies and American history.

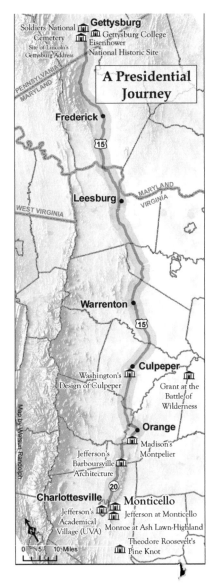

PRESIDENTIAL SITES ALONG THE JOURNEY THROUGH HALLOWED GROUND

1. Jefferson at Monticello
2. Jefferson's Academical Village
3. Monroe at Ash Lawn–Highland
4. Theodore Roosevelt's Pine Knot
5. Jefferson's Barboursville architecture
6. Madison's Montpelier
7. Grant at the Battle of Wilderness
8. Washington's Design of Culpeper
9. Monroe's Oak Hill Home
10. Camp David
11. Eisenhower National Historic Site
12. Lincoln at Gettysburg

Photo: Courtesy of Ash Lawn-Highland Home of James Monroe.

Few places outside Washington, D.C., are so closely associated with American presidents as The Journey Through Hallowed Ground. Many of the places along the Presidential Journey conjure images of the men, such as Lincoln at Gettysburg and Jefferson at Monticello. But this journey is more than the bricks and mortar of presidential places. Rarely, if ever, has there been such a chance to walk, literally, in their footsteps, and allow the landscape to influence your ponderings.

It's possible to imagine a time-warped moment when Madison, on his travels back from Philadelphia's constitutional debates over slavery, bumps into Lincoln as he delivers his Gettysburg Address. What words might they exchange?

Each of the sites is linked in some substantial way to a U.S. president. For example, George Washington laid out the original plat for the town of Culpeper, Virginia. While most sites are also described elsewhere in this guide, they are provided together here to offer another lens on the region and to enable you to create your own journey.

Begin at Monticello and nearby Ash Lawn–Highland just southeast of Charlottesville, Va.

Monticello, home of Thomas Jefferson. Thomas Jefferson was more than a statesman and founder of the United States. He was a renowned architect working in classical design, an innovative farmer and vintner, a fine arts promoter, and an advocate for world-class universities (and the founder of one). And Jefferson was a leading philosophical thinker of the early Federal period. Nowhere can you learn more about Jefferson beyond his presidency than at his home atop the mountain he called Monticello. Visitors can tour his gardens, plantation operation, and extraordinary home, which he designed and redesigned for nearly fifty years.

If you're interested in unparalleled scholastic resource materials, take an extra day to visit the Robert H. Smith International Center for Jefferson Studies. Located a quarter mile from the entrance to Monticello, on land once owned by Jefferson, the center is a residential site for individual Jefferson scholars and teachers, as well as a venue for lectures, seminars, and conferences. The Jefferson Library is also housed there. www.monticello.org/icjs.

Ash Lawn–Highland, home of President James Monroe. After serving as a soldier under George Washington in the American Revolution and crossing the Delaware River with him during the victorious Battle of Trenton, James Monroe became a Thomas Jefferson protégé in law and leadership. His home adjacent to Jefferson's Monticello, which he called Highland, is unique among presidential museums. Not only does it retell the life and times of the fifth president, it invites the public to truly experience the space the way Monroe enjoyed it. There are opera performances in the garden, cooking demonstrations, and educational opportunities. You can entertain your own friends there, if you wish—President Monroe's home is available for use by the public.

———

From Monroe's home, retrace your route back down the mountain to Route 20, Monticello Avenue. If you have made an appointment to visit Teddy Roosevelt's Pine Knot Cabin, turn left on Route 20 and proceed to Keene. For the University of Virginia Rotunda, turn right and follow Monticello Avenue into

The Virginia countryside. Photo: Steven L. Spring

Charlottesville to its end at Ridge Street. Turn right and follow to West Main Street. Turn left and watch for the signs to the University of Virginia.

Pine Knot Cabin, Theodore Roosevelt's woodland retreat. In May 1905, First Lady Edith Roosevelt purchased fifteen wooded acres south of Charlottesville as a retreat for the president. On the land was a twelve-foot by thirty-two-foot farm worker's cottage that had recently been built. She named it "Pine Knot" for the towering conifers surrounding the cottage and ordered alterations, such as the addition of chimneys and an outdoor privy. A spring provided water, which they carried to the cabin in buckets. Their total expenditure on the purchase and upgrades was $280. Over the next three years, the president and his family visited eight times to enjoy the rustic cabin. Mrs. Roosevelt later purchased an additional seventy-five acres adjacent to their land, but their visits to Pine Knot ended with the completion of Roosevelt's term of office. It is managed by the Edith and Theodore Roosevelt Pine Knot Foundation. Open by appointment. Tours can be arranged by

The Lawn and Rotunda at the University of Virginia.
Photo: Steven L. Spring

writing to the foundation at PO Box 213, Keene, VA 22946. www.pineknot.org.

Leaving Keene, travel north on Route 20 back to Charlottesville and follow the directions above.

The Rotunda at the University of Virginia, Thomas Jefferson, architect. It comes as a surprise to some to learn that the architect of the America Declaration of Independence is also the architect of one of the most classically beautiful buildings in America. What's more, the landscape around this building is considered one of the most inspired designs of public architecture anywhere. As the founder of the University of Virginia, Thomas Jefferson had a vision that extended beyond curricula. His term for the University of Virginia's campus was an "Academical Village." In addition to the Rotunda building, the original village includes a rectangular, terraced green space known as the Lawn, and two parallel rows of buildings—the Pavilions—connected by colonnaded walkways and student rooms. Together with Monticello, the site has been named a World Heritage Area—one of only twenty in the United States. Put it on the short list of places to see in your lifetime.

———

Leaving the university, retrace your route on West Main Street. At the downtown Mall, bear right onto Water Street (see Madison to Charlottesville section for information on dining). Watch for signs for Route 20 north. Travel fifteen miles through the rural Southwest Mountains Historic District into Orange County to arrive at Barboursville Vineyards. Follow the signs to the Barboursville Ruins.

Barboursville, Thomas Jefferson, architect. James Barbour was a Virginia governor, U.S. senator, diplomat, and cabinet secretary. He also was a friend of Thomas Jefferson. Jefferson designed a magnificent home north of Charlottesville for Barbour. Built between 1814 and 1822, it was widely known as one of the largest and finest houses in the region. Although it was destroyed by fire in 1884, the interior and exterior walls are still standing. Barboursville Vineyards now surround the ruins, which are open free to the public.

Barboursville Ruins. Photo : Steven L. Spring

From Barboursville, travel north on Route 20 eight miles to Montpelier.

James Madison's Montpelier. James Madison exemplifies a fact rarely heard today. In 1776, when he helped frame the new Virginia constitution, he was barely twenty-five years old. His friend Jefferson was in his early thirties. They were kids! Visiting Montpelier, Madison's lifelong home south of Orange, Virginia, you get to know how a young man becomes a voice for his state and, later, the nation. Montpelier was in the Madison family from 1723 to 1844, allowing a remarkable examination of life on a Virginia plantation. Madison's tomb is also at Montpelier.

Continue north on Route 20 into Orange (see Orange in the Madison to Charlottesville section for restaurants and attractions). Continue on Route 20 east; Wilderness Battlefield is nineteen miles from Orange.

Wilderness Battlefield, U.S. Grant in Command. This battle at the eastern end of Orange County is considered one of the most horrific of the entire Civil War. It is also considered a turning point in the war. It was May of 1864 and General U.S. Grant's first battle as commander of the Army of the Potomac. Here he faced Robert E. Lee for the first time. It was another victory for Lee and the Confederates. However, unlike Grant's predecessors, after the battle, Grant directed his army to continue toward Richmond rather than retreat—a first for the Union army. There is no visitor center here, but there is an interpretive shelter. In summer, a historian staffs the shelter to answer questions and lead programs.

From Wilderness, you can follow Route 3 northwest eighteen miles into Culpeper. Or, return to Orange and travel on Route 15 North.

Culpeper, George Washington, surveyor. In addition to its role in the Civil War (see Fauquier and Culpeper section), the town is linked to George Washington, who, as a young man, surveyed and platted the town's original lots and streets. For a two-day journey in the long days of summer, Culpeper is a convenient place to "bivouac" for the night.

The next site on the Presidential Journey is in Loudoun County. Travel north on Route 15, stopping to enjoy the town of Warrenton along the way.

Oak Hill, home of President James Monroe. James Monroe's Loudoun home was built 1822–24, while he served as president. It was here that Monroe retreated to formulate his administration's policy in a contentious debate over U.S. involvement in European wars and European colonization of the Americas. The document was his Annual Report to Congress, what we now call the annual State of the Union. In it, among other things, Monroe declared the Western Hemisphere off limits to European control. That policy later became known as the Monroe Doctrine. The house is a private residence, not open to the public, but noteworthy along the Journey.

———

Travel north on Route 15 through Leesburg and into Frederick County, Maryland. North of Frederick City, as the Catoctin Mountains dominate the view on the left, you are approaching Camp David. Because you can't stop there, plan to stop at the Cozy Restaurant in Thurmont to view its Camp David exhibit.

Camp David, a Presidential retreat. Located in Catoctin Mountain Park north of Frederick, Md., Camp David Presidential Retreat was established in 1942 by President Franklin Delano Roosevelt. He called the compound Shangri-La—the name of the mountain realm in the book *Lost Horizons.* It was a place for presidents to entertain away from the summer heat of Washington. President Eisenhower renamed it for his grandson in 1953. The many historic meetings held at Camp David include the planning of the Normandy invasion and the Camp David Accords. Its amenities include a driving range, putting green, and pool. Camp David is not open to the public, but there is a terrific exhibit in nearby Thurmont at the Cozy Restaurant—a hangout for White House aides and press corps when the president is at the retreat. Historic Cozy is a mile south of downtown Frederick on Frederick Road.

———

From Thurmont, continue north on Route 15 past Emmitsburg into Pennsylvania. Take the first exit onto Business Route 15 toward Gettysburg and the final three sites on this Presidential Journey.

David Wills House, Lincoln's Gettysburg Address. David Wills' house is on Lincoln Square in Gettysburg. Wills had invited President Lincoln to give a few "appropriate remarks" to dedicate the new Soldier's National Cemetery in Gettysburg, where soldiers who had died in the battle had been buried. Lincoln stayed with Wills on this site on the eve of his speech, delivered November 19, 1863. Lincoln is said to have completed the final edits of his speech, now known as the Gettysburg Address, at the Wills house. The building is owned by the National Park Service, which is planning a museum for the site to open in 2007.

Eisenhower National Historic Site, President Eisenhower's Home. As a career soldier, then U.S. president, Dwight D. Eisenhower and his wife Mamie had spent many years moving place to place. They purchased this farm adjacent to the battlefield at Gettysburg in 1950, the first home they had ever owned. During his presidency, the farm was a weekend retreat and a place for entertaining world leaders. After his presidency, they retired to the farm. Visitors get to see both the great general/president and the "regular guy" who raised cattle and enjoyed watching sit-coms on his television on the back porch. Tours of the farm leave from the visitor center at the Gettysburg battlefield.

Gettysburg College played a significant part in the battle of Gettysburg. Chartered in 1832, the campus of the then-named Pennsylvania College totaled three buildings and served a student body of little more than 100 young men. In July of 1863, the campus was thrown into the midst of the fight, providing shelter for the wounded and dying as a field hospital. In 1960, the president of Gettysburg College offered his on-campus home to former president Dwight D. Eisenhower as a post-presidential office. Ike served the college as a member of its Board of Trustees until his death in 1969. He wrote his memoirs and met with many heads of state in what is now known as Eisenhower House, which today holds the College's Admissions Offices.

Soldiers' National Cemetery, site of Lincoln's Gettysburg Address. Across from the Gettysburg battlefield, the cemetery was created for the thousands of soldiers who died in the Battle of Gettysburg. At the cemetery's dedication, November 19, 1863, Abraham Lincoln gave his legendary Gettysburg Address, one of the most celebrated speeches in the English language. An engraved memorial displays the text of the speech. The cemetery is open to the public free of charge.

2. African American Heritage Tour

Highlights: Museums, historical sites, and walking tours that interpret African American Heritage.

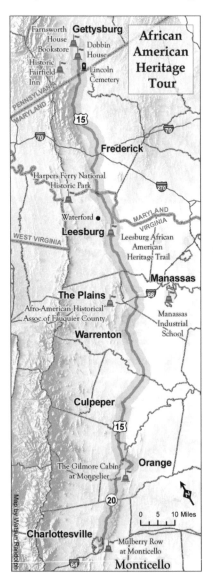

African American history is more than a story of an ethnic group. It's a window on America itself. Along The Journey Through Hallowed Ground, there are memorials, exhibits, and museums that recount the African American experience. Some sites are destinations all their own; others make for fascinating stops while touring the Journey. The locations of the sites are listed south to north and are described by proximity to Routes 15 or 20/231, the mainline of The Journey Through Hallowed Ground.

Mulberry Row at Monticello. Mulberry Row was a thousand-foot strand of cabins and workshops located at the Main House at Monticello, the home of Thomas Jefferson. There were dwellings for black and white workers on the row. Jefferson's commercial nail manufacturing shop was there, too. Five cabins were occupied by enslaved people who performed household chores, such as cooking and washing. The cabins were outfitted with dirt floors, wooden chimneys, and a few necessities, but no furnishings. Slaves who wanted chairs and tables had to earn money after working hours in order to purchase them. Since the 1970s, archaeological research has uncovered and interpreted Mulberry Row. There are interpretive signs along the row. Tours of this special exhibit, called "Plantation Community," offer an informative glimpse into the lives of the enslaved and free workers at Monticello. The tours run April 25 through October.

———

From Monticello, descend the mountain to Route 20 and turn right, following Monticello Road into Charlottesville, then north on Route 20 to the home of James Madison in Orange County.

The Gilmore Cabin at James Madison's Montpelier. There are two programs to learn about African American history at Montpelier. The Montpelier Enslaved Community Tour is a guided tour through the Madison estate. Stops include the sites of slave dwellings, the slave cemetery, blacksmith shop, and the mansion basement, where enslaved household servants lived. The tour touches on African American community life and offers observations about Madison and slavery. The hour-long tour is offered once each week, Saturday, 11:00 a.m., from April through October.

The **Gilmore Cabin** is a simple one-room cabin located a half mile from the Montpelier visitor center. The cabin's owner, George Gilmore, was born a slave at Montpelier in 1810. Like millions of other emancipated African Americans, he suddenly found himself with choices about where to live and how to make a living. George leased sixteen acres from Dr. James Madison, the president's great nephew, shortly after his emancipation, and in 1873 built the cabin that still stands. Like most subsistence farmers, white and black, Gilmore and each family member participated in the cash economy through part-time employment, small enterprises (such as his wife's work washing and mending clothes), and selling surplus farm goods. In 1901, he purchased the sixteen acres where he had been living for thirty-five years. Gilmore's descendents have assisted in archaeology and research at the farm. The interior of the cabin is open only on summer weekends, but you can tour the grounds all year.

———

In Prince William County, twelve miles east of Route 15 is the town of Manassas, best known for the two Civil War battles fought there. To reach Manassas traveling north, follow Route 29 from its junction with Route 15. Travel through Manassas Battlefield, then go south on Route 234.

Manassas Industrial School—Jennie Dean Memorial. Jane Serepta Dean founded the Manassas Industrial School for Colored Youth in 1894. Born a slave in Prince William County in 1852, Jennie Dean founded a school where young African American men and women could learn a trade and gain economic independence. The school was a residential institution offering both academic and vocational instruction. Frederick Douglas spoke at the dedication ceremony in 1894. The memorial is a four-acre park that contains a bronze model of the campus, interpretive markers, and a kiosk describing Dean's tireless efforts to raise money for the school. Historical markers outline some of the original buildings. Highlights include the photographs of students who attended the school between 1894 and 1966 and the audio program at the kiosk. 9601 Prince William St., Manassas, Va. Open daily, dawn to dusk; group tours available (and encouraged!). (703) 368-1873; www.manassas museum.org.

———

Retrace your route to Route 29, and turn left. At Gainesville, turn right on Route 55 to Haymarket. On the other side of town, cross over Route 15 and proceed twelve miles west to The Plains, Virginia.

Afro-American Historical Association of Fauquier County. Known for its genealogical resource center and educational programs, the organization features a marvelous exhibit space on

Loudoun County Courthouse. Photo: Judith P. Lillis

local, regional, and national African American history. Following footprints painted onto the floor, you begin in Africa in the 1600s and finish in the 1960s at lunch counters and public rallies. Along the way are newspaper articles, paintings, photographs, and artifacts that turn you from a detached observer of history into a neighbor of local families who still reside in the area. This museum is a treasure. While you're there, pick up a driving tour to African American churches in Fauquier County. The museum and archives are open Monday through Friday, 10 a.m.; Saturdays 1 to 5. 4249 Loudoun Ave.; (540) 253-7488.

Back on Route 15, head north into Loudoun County and Leesburg, where you can take a self-guided walking tour. Think of walking tours as storytelling in motion. Although some buildings along the way might be open to the public a few times each year, the tours are less about the buildings than about a lens through which you experience a place. For number of sites, depth of research, and quality of interpretation, the walking tours of Leesburg and Waterford are gems.

Leesburg African American Heritage Trail, a self-guided walking tour. Pick up a copy at the Loudoun Museum, 16 Loudoun St. SW, (703) 777-7427; or at the Balch Library, 208 W. Market St., (703) 737-7195, www.leesburgva.gov/services/library.

The tour takes you to cemeteries, streetscapes, and buildings—most of the buildings are not open to the public, but some are business locations and are open. Start at the Loudoun County Courthouse. This is where famed Civil Rights lawyer Charles Houston successfully made the case that "separate but equal" was far from equal. His appearance did not end segregated schools in Loudoun, but did lead to the establishment and construction of an African American high school in Loudoun, enabling black children to leave dilapidated one-room schools that lacked running water or heat.

There also is a building named for John W. Tolbert, who in the 1970s became the first African American elected to the Leesburg town council. The building, which was relocated to its current address, had been owned by a prominent African American family. It was preserved through Tolbert's leadership.

You can pause during this tour for coffee or to peek at antiques, art, and other offerings along the way.

There are two paths to Waterford. From downtown Leesburg, you can travel north on Route 608, Morven Park Road, which becomes Old Waterford Road at Morven Park. It's a windy, unpaved road—an altogether pleasant drive in dry weather. You can also go west on Route 7 four miles to Route 9. Go about a half mile on Route 9 and turn right onto Clarkes Gap Road.

Waterford. Request the *Share with Us* pamphlet from the Waterford Foundation; (540) 882-3018; www.waterfordva.org. The tiny village of **Waterford** was an anomaly in Virginia. Settled by Northern Quakers, Water-ford was founded on the principles of acceptance and equality. As the town grew, not all of the new landowners shared this worldview. So the town had both a large

Photo: CMW

free black population, some of whom owned property, and enslaved people. The Quaker commitment to education meant there were schools for black children—albeit sepa-rate ones—long before most Southern black children had schools. Actually, Waterford had them at a time when it was illegal to teach African Americans to read. It was known as a free town during the Civil War, a reputation that brought enmity from Confederate troops but did not spare it from the harassment of Northern troops.

The best time to take this tour is during the hugely popular annual Waterford Fair, the first weekend in October. Three stops along the tour are open to the public: the Second Street School, the John Wesley Church, and the Mill.

From Waterford, return to Route 9. Turn right and travel seven miles to Hillsboro. Two miles past Hillsboro, turn right onto Route 671, Harpers Ferry Road. Follow this road eight miles to its end at Route 340. Turn left at the light, cross the Shenandoah River and go up the hill to the traffic light. Turn left into the Harpers Ferry NHP visitor center.

Harpers Ferry National Historical Park. Through the life of one little town on the Potomac River, you learn about industrial history beginning in the early nineteenth century, slavery and the Civil War, and the founding of the modern Civil Rights movement.

There are six major exhibits at the park devoted to African American history. The John Brown museum includes artifacts, storyboards, and video presentations charting the history of slavery and the abolitionist movement. There also is a section of the iron fence from the firehouse. It is massive, about seven feet tall. It's not stowed behind ropes or barriers; it's right there to touch, positioned in front of a mural of the firehouse where Brown's men holed up. You grab onto that fence, you see the doomed would-be liberators on the other side, and you can't help but ponder: what would I have done? Upstairs is an the Allies of Freedom exhibit about the five black men who participated in John Brown's raid—four of whom died in battle or were later hanged.

Also in Harpers Ferry's lower town are Black Voices and the Storer College Niagara Movement exhibits. Black Voices is an interactive display built on the stories of local Harpers Ferry residents in the days before emancipation. There are several exhibits, each depicting one person's story. After reading a short storyboard introducing that person's account, you pick up a telephone to hear a narrator relay the story in first person. The exhibit unsettles you in a surprising way: the experience is one of being on the phone, listening to a neighbor break your heart with a story about an injustice visited upon another neighbor.

Across the street is the Storer College Niagara Exhibit. Storer College operated from 1870 until 1955 in Harpers Ferry. One of its students would later become the first president of Nigeria. And the great jazz arranger Don Redman, who also was a leading developer of swing and the big band sound, attended Storer.

The college hosted the 1906 meeting of the Niagara Movement, founded by W.E.B. Du Bois. It was the group's second meeting,

Harpers Ferry National Historical Park.
Photo: Courtesy of Harpers Ferry National Historical Park

and its first meeting on American soil. Their first meeting was hastily moved across the Niagara River into Canada the previous year because no hotel in Buffalo would have the delegation. The meeting is considered by many as the beginning of the modern Civil Rights era. Its members would help launch the NAACP a few years later.

There are more exhibits on the 1906 Niagara meeting and Civil Rights at the Storer College Campus, now a National Park Service training facility. In the main building, Mather Training Center, is a remarkable photographic exhibit of the meeting and the people behind the movement. If you want to walk in the footsteps of history, take the walk from the visitor center to the Murphy Farm. In 1906, the Niagara delegates walked from Storer College to John Brown's Fort, which had been dismantled and moved to the farm by the Murphy family. It's a two-mile round trip stroll, with the added bonus of a vista offering one of the finest views of the Shenandoah River. www.nps.gov/hafe.

From Harpers Ferry, retrace your route on Route 340, but do not turn back onto Route 671 at the bottom of the hill. Stay on Route 340 toward Frederick. Five miles from Frederick, Route 15 joins 340. At Frederick, go north on Route 15. Gettysburg is about a half hour up the road.

Lincoln Cemetery. The cemetery is on Long Lane in Gettysburg. Coming into town on Baltimore Street, go left on Breckenridge, then left on Long Lane. An organization of African American men called the Sons of Good Will established the cemetery in 1867 for the burial of Gettysburg's Civil War veterans, who were denied burial in the National Cemetery. Thirty Civil War veterans are buried here. In 1906, when housing development uprooted the town's other black cemetery, the remains were transferred here and the cemetery renamed Lincoln Cemetery. www.brotherswar.com/These_Honored_Dead-7c.htm

----

While in Gettysburg, there are three businesses with an African American heritage connection. Two are restaurants with Underground Railroad interpretive exhibits. The other is a comfortable bookstore with a first-rate collection on the African American experience.

Dobbin House Restaurant. Just a short walk from the battlefield visitor center in Gettysburg, the Dobbin House was a station on the Underground Railroad. There is an exhibit room upstairs featuring artifacts uncovered during an archaeological dig. In the museum room, up a narrow staircase, is an Underground Railroad exhibit. Beyond a false bookshelf and behind the wall are three life-sized wax figures, two adults and a child. They are crouched into a space that allows just enough room to sit. The Dobbin House staff will direct you to the exhibit. While there, have lunch in the cozy Springhouse Tavern downstairs. 89 Steinwehr Ave.; (717) 334-2100; www.dobbinhouse.com.

Farnsworth House Bookstore. Farnsworth House is well known for its food, tavern, overnight guest rooms, and entertaining ghost stories. It also has a bookstore specializing in Civil War and World War Two books, both new and out-of-print. The shop has a large inventory of books on the African American experience through the Antebellum and Civil War eras. 401 Baltimore St. Open daily. (717) 334-8838; www.farnsworthhouseinn.com.

Historic Fairfield Inn. The inn is said to have been a station on the Underground Railroad. Restaurant patrons are invited to view a hiding place discovered behind second-story walls that the innkeepers have preserved as an unadorned exhibit. Order lunch in Squire Miller's Tavern or dinner in the Mansion House; explore the place while you await your meal. Fairfield is eight miles west of Gettysburg on Route 116.

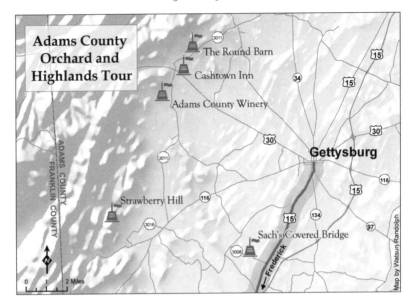

3. Adams County, PA.
Orchards and Highlands Loop

Highlights: The Journey begins at a covered bridge and visits a stop on the Underground Railroad. There are breathtaking views of Adams County's Orchard Belt nestled below South Mountain, and a stop at one of the Journey's architectural wonders, the Historic Round Barn and Farm Market in Cashtown. While on the way, you can stop at a scenic winery and follow A.P. Hill's steps along Old Route 30 to the front porch (or the pub) of the Cashtown Inn.

Distance: 45 miles.

From Lincoln Square, follow Springs Avenue four blocks, climbing Seminary Ridge, to the intersection with Confederate Avenue/Seminary Ridge. Turn left, and after crossing Route 116, continue about two miles south on West Confederate Avenue, which borders the western edge of the battlefield. In addition to monuments, there is an observation tower from which to view the Union line.

Turn right onto Millerstown Road (which becomes Pumping Station Road), passing the Eisenhower National Historic Site on the left—tours of the Eisenhower Farm depart from the battlefield visitor center. Just after crossing Marsh Creek, turn left onto Scotts Road and go about two hundred yards to the bridge parking area.

Sach's Covered Bridge. Take some time to wander on the bridge, noting the intricate lattice work construction. Built in 1852, Sach's Bridge is more than a charming artifact. Standing on the bridge, you can imagine the caissons and cannon rumbling over the wooden planks. The bridge was preserved by the Gettysburg Battlefield Preservation Association and is on the National Register of Historic Places. www.gbpa.org.

———

To continue, turn left on Pumping Station Road and enjoy the view of tidy Adams County farmland. In about 1.5 miles, turn right onto Camp Gettysburg Road. Then at Route 116, turn left toward Fairfield. As you approach Fairfield, the Appalachians appear on the horizon. Just outside the village of Fairfield, turn right onto Carroll Tract Road, then take the first left onto Mt. Hope Road.

Strawberry Hill. Morton Salt heiress Frances Morton Froelicher and her husband Hans purchased Strawberry Hill as a rustic retreat in 1960. Today, Strawberry Hill Nature Center and Preserve encompasses more than six hundred acres of mountain streams below Mount Hope. (See Adams County, Exploring the Countryside.)

———

Return to Route 116, and turn right into the village of Fairfield. In addition to the Historic Fairfield Inn, there is a casual Italian/ pizza place, an authentic little diner, and, at the far end of town on the left, a quiet coffee shop serving terrific sandwiches.

———

After a stroll in Fairfield, backtrack on Route 116 to Camp Gettysburg Road and turn left onto Knoxlyn Road, passing the lovely Lower Marsh Presbyterian Church, built in 1790. In 1.4 miles, turn left onto Knoxlyn-Orrtanna and soon enter orchard country, where rolling hills stretch into the distance. A fixture of the Adams County landscape for centuries, the Orchard Belt's growers are being overwhelmed by imported fruit. If you like the view, eat some apples available at the family orchards along the drive.

At the Knouse Food Cooperative, turn right on Orrtanna Road and follow it for about two miles to a four-way stop. Turn left onto Scott School Road. The immediate right is Bingaman Road— you will return to this after a stop at Adams County Winery. Follow the signs.

Adams County Winery. At the end of a country lane, the winery is a scenic spot for a tasting and a picnic. You can purchase snacks for a fancy picnic under the pines. See Gettysburg, Exploring the Countryside.

———

Leaving the winery, backtrack to Bingaman Road and turn left. You'll need to pull over to enjoy the views of South Mountain and Cashtown Pass above the endless orchards. In two miles, reach Old Route 30. Turn right and follow the same road Confederate columns took into Gettysburg. About two miles down the road, you can stop for a rest where the troops bivouacked

Cashtown Inn. The inn has been serving travelers coming through the pass since 1797. It served as the Gettysburg headquarters for Confederate General A.P. Hill. There are gardens to stroll and a porch for sitting. For a special treat on a summer's day, have a glass of the house raspberry iced tea out on the porch swing. (See Adams County, Lodging.)

———

At High Street, turn left and proceed across Route 30 to the Round Barn Market on Cashtown Road.

The Round Barn. This architectural marvel was built at the height of the round barn era in 1914. Now owned by Knouse Fruitlands, the barn is a market for a huge variety of fruits, berries, vegetables, and an assortment of jams and other farm bounty. Stop by in autumn for cider pressing. Kids enjoy the farm animals outside. Men just like looking at the barn. (717) 334-1984; www.roundbarngettysburg.com.

If you're totally wiped out at this point, you can follow Route 30 east back into Gettysburg, but you will miss incredible scenery. To continue on the scenic drive, follow Route 30 west two miles to Route 234 (Buchanan Valley Road). Turn right, then take an immediate right onto Church Road. Follow Church Road over Mount Newman, past the quaint St. Ignatius Loyola Church, built in 1816, to rejoin Buchanan Valley Road in about three miles.

Turn right and follow Route 234 for nine miles to Biglerville, home of the National Apple Museum (Saturdays and Sundays in season). En route, you will pass through the Narrows of Conewago Creek, a deep-cut gorge where the water races and creates one of the finest picnic spots in Adams County. In Biglerville, turn right onto Route 34 and go seven miles back into Gettysburg for a cup of coffee or an afternoon libation on Lincoln Square.

4. Catoctin Scenic Loop

Highlights: This is your chance to travel not just along The Journey Through Hallowed Ground, but *into* it—into the mountains, that is, to enjoy stunning views of Frederick County. Follow a leafy drive through the Catoctin Mountains to the famed Cunningham Falls and the historical exhibits at Catoctin Mountain Park, then on to historic Thurmont for lunch and the Camp David exhibit at Historic Cozy. From there, spend time explor-ing Catoctin Furnace before a scenic return to Frederick via a covered bridge.

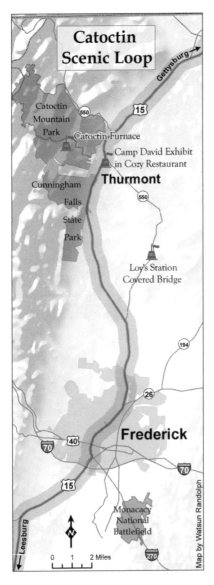

Distance:
About 35 miles
County:
Frederick

Leaving historic downtown on Patrick Street, then following Route 144 a mile from town onto Route 40, pass through the mile-long commercial stretch and stay right where Alternate Route 40 bears left. A quarter mile further, the giant candy cane marks the spot. You don't really have to look for it; you'll see it on the right.

Breakfast at Barbara Fritchie "Candy Stick" Restaurant.
No need for faux nostalgia here; this place is what those modern
diners are trying to emulate. It's a family-run business that's been
dishing up home cooking and baking since 1910. Breakfast is
available all day. So is pie. 1513 W. Patrick St.; (U.S. Route 40);
(301) 662-2500.

———

From the Candy Stick, turn right and climb into the hills. Go
about five miles, then turn right onto Gambrill Park Road. The
road winds into mountains, entering Gambrill State Park. At the
top of the hill, you can pull into High Knob picnic area for
spectacular views from the pavilion, then continue north.

The Catoctin range is a kind of Central Park for Frederick
County, with some twenty thousand acres of parks and forest
stretching from Route 40 more than twenty miles north—almost
to the Pennsylvania line. Stay on Gambrill Park for several miles
until the junction with Tower Road. Go left here—if you want to
climb a lookout tower for more great views, detour right on Gambrill
Park Road for a half mile. Stay on Tower Road for one mile, then
turn right onto Mink Farm Road. A mile further, Mink Farm Road
ends at Catoctin Hollow Road.

Turn left and drive through the forest, coming to Cunningham
Falls State Park. Follow signs for Falls parking.

Cunningham Falls. At seventy-eight feet, this cascading
waterfall surely ranks as one of the great natural features along The
Journey Through Hallowed Ground. What's more, its location only
three miles from Thurmont makes it one of the most accessible
ones as well. Parking and picnic tables are located at Hunting Creek
Lake. There also is a handicap-accessible lot on Route 77.

———

Turn east (right) onto Route 77 toward Thurmont, and travel
one mile to the Catoctin Mountain Park visitor center.

Catoctin Mountain Park. In the 1920s and 1930s, most eastern mountain ranges were nearly treeless. Timber harvesting and charcoal production had led to soil erosion into creeks and streams. So launched the era of national and state forests and watershed reserves. In the Catoctin Mountains, the federal government started an ambitious demonstration program to regenerate the forest. This is also the time that President Roosevelt established the presidential retreat in these mountains—today's Camp David. The plan was to turn over all of the federal land to the state of Maryland for parkland. Whether Roosevelt just fancied the land as a national park or whether creation of the presidential retreat created security issues is a matter for historians to debate. But the result is two fine parks, one state and one national, split by Route 77.

The visitor center at Catoctin Park houses a modest but informative display on the natural and cultural heritage of the mountains. You can drive up Central Park Road to a short trail interpreting the charcoal operations that dominated the mountain and provided fuel for Catoctin Furnace. There is a bookstore that carries maps and local histories; there also is a restroom.

———

Continue east on Route 77 into Thurmont, a historic Maryland Main Street community. You can stroll the entire town before lunch (see Thurmont, Eating Out). Turn right on Water Street, then right on Frederick Road to the Historic Cozy.

Cozy Restaurant and the Camp David Exhibit. The Camp David exhibit displays memorabilia, photographs, news clippings––all nicely done. It's a worthy stop, made even more so by the fact that it's inside the Cozy: a slightly whacky world unto itself where you would enjoy wandering around even if they didn't also serve food and libations in eleven distinctly themed dining rooms. Order lunch and have a look around.

———

Heading south, Frederick Road becomes Catoctin Furnace Road. The furnace is only a mile from town.

Catoctin Furnace. Catoctin Furnace is part of Cunningham Falls State Park. Only one blast furnace and the ruins of the manager's residence remain. Storyboards describe the iron era history of the region and the Civil War action that took place nearby. It's a fifteen-minute stop that will greatly enlarge your view of the surrounding landscape. And it's free. www.dnr.state.md.us/publiclands/cunninghamguide.html.

————

Head back into Thurmont and turn right onto Main Street, Route 77. At the eastern edge of town, bear left to stay on Route 77, now Rocky Ridge Road, and enjoy the scenic valley. In two miles, reach Old Frederick Road. Turn right to reach the covered bridge.

Loy's Station Covered Bridge Park. Constructed in 1848, the bridge has been rebuilt but its original timbers are in tact over the ninety-foot span across Owens Creek. There are picnic tables in the adjacent park.

————

Continue south on Old Frederick Road, which rejoins Route 15 just north of Frederick.

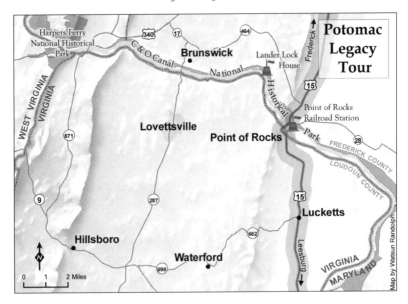

5. Potomac Legacy Loop

Highlights: A scenic drive in Loudoun, Va., Frederick and Washington, Md., with a stop in Harpers Ferry, W.Va. Cross the Potomac River at the site of a Civil War skirmish, then take a scenic drive upriver to Brunswick, Md., and on to Harpers Ferry, W.Va. The return passes through the historic Loudoun villages of Hillsboro and Waterford, with stops at three vineyards.

Distance: 50 miles

Travel north on Route 15 out of Leesburg, taking a moment to investigate the Civil War Trails marker on Tutt Lane, north of the bypass junction—turn left and drive a quarter mile to the marker. Back on Route 15 North, you will pass through the crossroads village of Lucketts, where antiques and collectable shops draw you to stop a while. Four miles further, cross the bridge into Point of Rocks, Maryland, named for the striking outcrop that captures your view as you cross the river.

Point of Rocks Railroad Station. Built in 1875, the station demonstrates the primacy of railroads in the decades following the

Civil War. It ranks among the best examples of Victorian Gothic Revival public architecture. The station is a commuter stop on the MARC line to Washington, D.C. Although the interior of the building is not open to the public, the exterior calls out for a photograph.

———

Continue on Route 15 one mile, and turn left onto Route 464, Point of Rocks Road, en route to Brunswick. Halfway there, if you turn left onto Lander Road, you can visit a bit of history along the C&O Canal.

Lander Lock House, Lander, Md. During the canal era, from 1828 to 1924, lockkeepers were on duty twenty-four hours each day, seven days a week. They received a small salary and small house. This house was restored through the efforts of volunteers, who also have raised money to maintain the structure. Take a walk or a ride along the C&O Canal towpath while you're there. The lock house is open and staffed by volunteers on weekends in summer only. You can see it from the outside daily. 2800 Lander Road on the C&O Canal; (301) 834-4044.

———

Continue on Route 464 to the outskirts of Brunswick. Turn right at the traffic light by the high school, then left at the next light onto Route 17, Petersville Road, which leads to downtown.

Brunswick

Brunswick is an old railroad town that doesn't make its way into many travel guides. Too bad. In addition to having the C&O Canal and a lovely train station (now serving MARC passengers), Brunswick has a walkable Main Street and an increasing number of stops to please travelers—including a café in a former church building. The Brunswick Railroad Museum alone demands a detour into town. There are a handful of antique and second-hand shops that are, like the rest of the town, unpretentious and priced just right.

🏛 HISTORICAL SITES AND HERITAGE MUSEUMS

Brunswick Railroad Museum. Once a canal town called Berlin, Brunswick was built around one of the largest rail yards in the B&O system. At one point, every freight train passing through the region came first to Brunswick for "sorting," kind of like today's overnight delivery service sending every package to one airport. It is somewhat limiting to refer to this as a railroad museum because it is as much a glimpse into early twentieth- century America as it is a recollection of the role of rail. The museum is welcoming to kids, too. The "Hands on History" exhibit lets young kids run the railroad—and lets parents look at other exhibits while they're at it. Anyone interested in regional history can while away hours at the scale model of the B&O metropolitan subdivision. 40 West Potomac St. Open Fridays, 10 to 2; Saturdays, 10 to 4; Sundays, 1 to 4. www.brrm.net.

C&O Canal National Historical Park. Truly one of America's most interesting national parks, it is rich in history and offers easy, barrier-free hiking and biking. The towpath is just beyond the train station, and the visitor center for the C&O Canal is adjacent to the Brunswick Railroad Museum; open during museum hours. www.nps.gov/choh.

🎁 DISTINCTIVE SHOPS AND STOPS

Antiques, etc. Talk about recycling! There are three shops in town, with the tone set by Antiques n' Ole Stuff, 25 E. Potomac St. Although you can find fine antiques on the floor, there is nothing highbrow going on here, just quality old furniture, books, record albums, lamps, and other things. Cripple Creek Antiques, 24 W. Potomac, and Past and Present, 20 W. Potomac, offer similar, albeit fewer bargains.

Beans in the Belfry. The kind of place everyone wants in their neighborhood. Set in a historic church building, there are comfy chairs, conversation areas set apart by old doors and windows, a choir loft, and historical relics lying about for your examination. The coffee is organic, and there is a fine menu of soups, sandwiches, and pastries. It's a kid friendly place (and, dude, it's got free wireless internet). Perhaps best of all, there is live music on weekends and a Sunday jazz brunch. Open 8 a.m. to 9 p.m. 122 W. Potomac St.; (301) 834-7178; www.beansinthebelfry.com.

Book Crossing. This charming shop is in the old downtown pharmacy. The proprietors have retained the original cabinetry, counters, tile floor, and other accouterments of a trusted local druggist's shop. Just as they did in generations past, Brunswick youngsters still wander in for candy after school, now stored in the old wooden drawers. Visitors to Brunswick appreciate the café seating for sipping tea or a freshly brewed cuppa while browsing periodicals or combing through the books on local history or by local authors. If you're visiting Brunswick to take your kids to the Railroad Museum, stop by Book Crossing to see if the shop has any children's programs scheduled for the day. 2 E. Main St.; (301) 834-5577; www.thebookcrossing.biz

Kings Pizza. A family-run operation that serves up a divine spinach pie, pizza, and Italian sandwiches and entrees. 215 W. Potomac St. (301) 834-9999

———

Leave Brunswick by driving out West Potomac Street. Pass through the crossroads village of Knoxville, and take the ramp onto Route 340 South—watch for high-speed traffic on the right as you enter. Ahead of you are terrific views of the Blue Ridge at Harpers Ferry Gap. To visit Harpers Ferry, continue on Route 340, cross the Potomac and Shenandoah rivers, and proceed to the traffic light at the top of the hill. Turn left into the visitor center for a quick shuttle ride to the town.

Harpers Ferry National Historical Park, Harpers Ferry, W.Va. A unique park in a dramatic setting, Harpers Ferry shows how one town came to play a significant role in history. There is a long list of historical figures with a Harpers Ferry connection, from Meriwether Lewis, Thomas Jefferson, and George Washington to John Brown, Frederick Douglas, and W.E.B. Du Bois. At the same time, the everyday lives of the town's inhabitants become the backdrop for stories of industrial history, the Civil War, and civil rights.

The park itself is housed in a collection of historic buildings, each an exhibit on one element of the town's history. For example, the John Brown museum traces the history of slavery and the raid on Harpers Ferry; the Industrial Museum describes early manufacturing that took place here. You can cross the footbridge into Maryland to walk along the C&O Canal towpath or hike up Maryland Heights for distant views of the surrounding countryside.

The park is located in an extraordinary setting where the Piedmont meets the Blue Ridge, at the confluence of the Shenandoah and Potomac rivers. The park and commercial establishments comfortably share the Lower Town to promote the experience that you are actually walking around in a living historical space.

After touring Harpers Ferry, retrace your driving route across the Shenandoah River. Just before the Potomac (at the gas station), turn right on Route 671, Harpers Ferry Road. This scenic valley between Short Hill and the Blue Ridge is called Between the Hills. If you haven't had a proper walk yet, you can stop at the Blue Ridge Center for Environmental Stewardship, where there are ten miles of trails (see Loudoun County, Outdoor Recreation). At the end of Harpers Ferry Road is the first of three wineries.

Three Hillsboro Wineries

Breaux Vineyards. The Breaux family began producing wines as a hobby and realized they had a hit on their hands; it was time to produce commercially. The wines produced at the 404-acre estate have become some of Virginia's best known, as have the popular events. The annual Cajun weekend is one of the larger draws in the region. Located one mile from the intersection of Routes 9 and 761; (540)668-6299; www.breauxvineyards.com.

Leaving Breaux Vineyards, turn left toward Route 9. At the traffic light, turn left. Hillsborough Vineyards is about a half mile on the left.

Hillsborough Winery. The tasting room in the 1840 stone barn is a captivating spot. Full of light and wood, it's a difficult place to leave. Get a bottle and a couple of glasses, and head outside to a pond with the sound of trickling waterfalls. 36716 Charles Town Pike; (540) 668-6216; www.hillsboroughwine.com.

Go left from the winery and pass through the tiny village of Hillsboro—the home, says the sign at the edge of town, of Wilbur and Orville Wright's mother. Turn left on Mountain Road and go about a mile to the winery.

Windham Winery. The tasting room is in a barn set in a scenic valley. From the glass-enclosed porch grounds you see beautiful views of a pond and Short Hill. There are twelve acres of vineyards on this five-hundred-acre farm, an inviting place for a picnic and to watch the birds from the deck. The cabernet franc is especially popular. 14727 Mountain Rd.; (540) 668-6464; www.windhamwinery.com.

Back on Route 9, travel east five miles to the blinking light at Hamilton Station Road. Go left and drive to the end of the road. Turn left. At the entrance to Waterford, turn left on Factory Street and proceed into the village.

Waterford. Perhaps the most surprising thing about Waterford is that it exists at all. The village grew up around Amos Janney's mill on Catoctin Creek, after Janney and other Quakers arrived in the early 1730s. Remarkably, the integrity of the village is still intact, looking much the way it looked in the mid-nineteenth century. But it's a lot quieter now than it was then. By the 1830s, there was a tannery, chair maker, boot manufacturer, shops, and a tavern. Today, behind the houses on Second and Main streets, instead of a grid of early twentieth-century streets or a cluster of twenty-first-century cul de sacs, there are sheep grazing on the famed grasses of Loudoun. The town is a National Historic Landmark.

If you stop at the offices of the Waterford Foundation at the corner of Second and Main, you can pick up a walking guide to the historic buildings—which in Waterford, means all the buildings. You can also pick up a copy of *Share With Us*, a walking guide to the village's African American history. As a Quaker town espousing freedom and equality, most of Waterford's black population was not enslaved. Officially, the village did not secede from the Union at the outbreak of the Civil War. Instead, it eventually recruited Virginia's only unit to serve in the Union army.

The only commerce in town is a tiny grocery, which means don't drive into Waterford looking for dinner. Come for an afternoon stroll through a peaceful historic village. The main event in town is the annual Waterford Homes Tour & Crafts Exhibit the first weekend each October, billed as the oldest juried craft show in Virginia. www.waterfordva.org.

———

From Waterford, retrace your route out of the village. Instead of turning right onto Hamilton Station Road (Route 662 south), continue to the traffic light at Route 9. Go left and reach Route 7. Leesburg is a couple of miles east on Route 7.

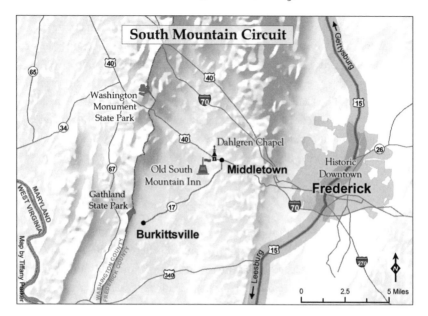

6. South Mountain Circuit

Highlights: Retrace the Battle of South Mountain in Frederick County, following back roads and mountain passes to towns and monuments.

Distance: 40 miles

Traveling west from Frederick, the route follows Route 180, which roughly parallels Route 340 but provides an altogether different perspective. In the little town of Jefferson is Jefferson Pastry Shoppe, the regionally famous bakery. The bear claws, Danish, and donuts have been touted far and wide, but if morning sweets are not for you, you can pick up a loaf of bread or a pie for later. The pastry shop shares a parking lot with Hemp Meats, a butcher shop. You can pick up cheese to go with that bread.

Just past the bakery, turn right onto Old Middletown Road and follow the roller-coaster topography of the Middletown Valley. The road joins Route 17 as it enters Middletown. Turn left onto Route 40 Alternate and park.

Middletown, Md. During the Battle of South Mountain, there were major troop movements involving both armies. Among the main attractions here are a stroll past stately homes on Main Street, east of the intersection with Church Street, and the Zion Lutheran Church. The Central Maryland Heritage League, at 200 W. Main, is restoring Lamar House, location of a turn-of-the-century rural medical sanitarium. The site preserves Dr. Lamar's operating and recovery rooms, library, and medical equipment. www.cmhl.org. There is a diner and café just uphill from Lamar House.

Continue west on Route 40-A, a scenic road heading directly toward the ridge. A few miles from Middletown, Route 40-A completes a twisty final ascent to the top of South Mountain at Turner's Gap, where the Appalachian Trail crosses. Here are three notable sites: Dahlgren Chapel, Washington Monument, and South Mountain Inn.

Dahlgren Chapel. The chapel was built in 1881 by Sarah Madeleine Vinton Dahlgren, whose former summer home is now South Mountain Inn. The chapel was purchased and restored by the Central Maryland Heritage League. The chapel is open by appointment only, but the chapel's site in Turner's Gap makes even outdoor access worth the trip. To request an appointment: (301) 371-7090; www.cmhl.org.

Old South Mountain Inn. The Mountain House, now South Mountain Inn, dates to at least 1769, when Jacob Young purchased the land—other accounts affix a much earlier date for a tavern business on the site. It had been owned by Robert Turner, who purchased the land in 1750. It was the summer home of Madeleine Dahlgren. Its second incarnation as a tavern and restaurant dates to 1925. Today, the tavern is known for fine dining in a Colonial atmosphere; Sunday brunch is particularly popular. Saturday lunch in the President's Lounge is informal and relaxing.

Washington Monument State Park. The main attraction of this 108-acre park is the milk-jug shaped stone monument to the first president. The views from the top of the monument are wondrous, as Civil War scouts from both armies could attest. To reach the monument, you can drive the 1.5 miles from Route 40-A, but a nice walk along the Appalachian Trail is highly recommended. Services: concession and restrooms. www.dnr.state.md.us/publiclands/western/Washington.

———

Continue west on Route 40-A for a quarter mile, then turn left onto Moser Road. Go one mile and turn left onto Reno Mountain Road. At a monument to General Jesse Reno, the combat that occurred in Fox Gap during the Battle of South Mountain is interpreted. Continuing east down the mountain, Reno Monument Road joins Bolivar Road, then Marker Road. Turn right onto Marker and follow to a right turn on Mountain Church Road. The road ends at Main Street, Burkittsville. Turn left.

Burkittsville, Md. This lovely town nestled below South Mountain was settled at about the time of the American Revolution. It is remarkably well preserved. It was the site of the Battle of Crampton's Gap, the subject of a fine walking tour of the town. The tour can be downloaded from www.co.frederick.md.us/Burkittsville/civil.htm.

———

To complete the South Mountain circuit, drive into the mountain on Main Street, which becomes Gapland Road. As the road ascends, there are views of Pleasant Valley to the east. At the top, in Crampton's Gap, is Gathland State Park.

Gathland State Park. The park is the former mountain home of George Alfred Townsend, a Civil War journalist and novelist.

He was known as Gath. The estate has a quirky, interesting collection of buildings and structures designed by Townsend, not the least of which is the War Correspondence Memorial arch—thought to be the only monument to Civil War journalists. The park has a visitor center and picnic area—and the park is, indeed, a fine location for a picnic. The park includes all of Crampton's Gap, which was the southern most gap fought over during the battle of South Mountain. Services: concession and restrooms.

———

Return to Burkittsville and turn right onto south Route 17, which leads to Route 340 and a return to Frederick. To visit downtown Brunswick (see Potomac Heritage Loop), cross Route 340 and follow the signs into town.

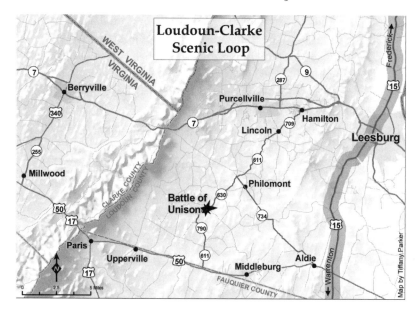

7. Loudoun–Clarke Scenic Loop

Highlights: If you enjoy bookstores, old mills, and country drives, this is a splendid trip. It is a day-long excursion into scenic Western Loudoun, with a brief sojourn into rural Clarke County for a visit to a working gristmill. Stops include historic Middleburg, a wonderful bookstore and small museum in Berryville, sunset overlooking the Shenandoah Valley at Bears Den, and dinner in Purcellville.

Distance: 45 miles

Begin the tour from downtown Leesburg, traveling west on Loudoun Street. Just before it merges with Market Street, turn left on Dry Mill Road. Follow Dry Mill out of town as it winds its way through the countryside until it ends at Route 7 (alternately, you could follow the four-lane Route 7 to this location). Follow Business 7 west into Hamilton.

Stop at Natural Mercantile as you enter Hamilton to pick up snacks for the drive. This natural food store has an extensive selection of earthy-crunchy, granola-fied goodness, along with organic chips, salsas, and juices. Stock up. If you're ready for a stroll, Hamilton's Main Street is just long enough to stretch your legs.

Continue west on Business Route 7 through Purcellville (you'll be back at day's end), and turn left on 20th Street; follow this several blocks to Robey Rd. Turn left and travel past Blue Ridge Middle School, then right on Route 722, Lincoln Road, to the village of Lincoln. This picturesque little village was founded by Quakers in the 1720s and still retains an air of solitude. The many historic buildings include the Quaker meetinghouse next to the post office. Beginning at the post office, there is a 3.5 dirt road loop around town. It passes historic homes and barns, and makes for a pleasing short bike ride.

———

Heading south from Lincoln, stay right to remain on Route 722. Just outside town, turn right onto Route 709, Chappelle Hill Road. Go straight at the junction with Route 611, then bear left to stay on Telegraph Springs Road. Follow this a few miles to Snickersville Turnpike. Turn left and follow one of the most scenic

Horse country in and around Loudoun County, Virginia.
Photo: Mike DeHart

roads of the Piedmont. The little crossroads village of Philomont, with its old country store, is just ahead.

To take a short detour to the Battle of Unison site, turn right on JEB Stuart Road in Philomont. Unison was the site of a significant Civil War battle in 1862. After the Battle of Antietam, Union General McClellan gave chase into Northern Virginia. General J.E.B. Stuart put up resistance in and around Unison. Vastly outnumbered, the Confederate troops held off the Union advance for three days. This gave General Longstreet time to reinforce Richmond and be in a position to defend Fredericksburg.

Back in Philomont, continue driving southeast on Snickersville Turnpike, crossing over Beaverdam Creek and Goose Creek. Just west of the village of Aldie is a wayside marker on the 1862 Battle of Aldie, a four-hour fight involving mounted assaults and close fighting.

At Route 50, turn left to visit Aldie (see Loudoun section), or turn right to continue on to Middleburg.

Middleburg

It's okay; admit it. You heard Middleburg and you thought, what? Staid, expensive, formal? Take another look. Some say it's got the finest New York pizza southa da City, as well as a microbrew pub grilling up brats and burgers, an Irish pub with a billiard room, and a whacky rambling don't-know-what-to-call-it store that sells everything from children's games to fine table linens. Also, think organic ice cream served in a second-floor loft of an old bank building. Actually, come to think of it, think three scoop shops in this little town—two of them serving up homemade.

Yes, you can find the finer things, plenty of them. Fashionable clothing and accessories, fine arts and prints, home décor—but even among these you can find bargains.

The best place to start a Middleburg ramble is at the Pink Box visitor center. In this tiny early nineteenth-century building, you can obtain a walking-tour guide and travel information. Take some time to view the collection of historic photographs—many of them by noted photographer Harold Allen. With walking tour booklet in hand, you can set off in any direction you please, using the booklet when one building or another cries out for explanation.

📖 WALKING TOURS HIGHLIGHTS

Jacqueline Kennedy Pavilion. A small memorial in a quiet pocket park acknowledges Jacqueline Kennedy Onassis' long association with Middleburg. She and President Kennedy favored Middleburg as a weekend retreat. She stabled her horses in the area, riding with two local hunts, and later rented a small cottage in the area. Next to Pink Box, 12 N. Madison St.

Civil War Horse sculpture on Vine Hill. The 1813 Federal-style mansion atop Vine Hill is a Middleburg landmark. Among its incarnations was the office of the *Chronicle of the Horse* and the National Sporting Library. The sculpture remembers the 1.5 million horses and mules killed or wounded in the Civil War. Paul Mellon commissioned the work by Tessa Pullan. 301 W. Washington St.

National Sporting Library, on Vine Hill, is in a new building reminiscent of an old carriage house. A one-of-a-kind research facility for turf and field sports, the library houses a collection of thirteen thousand books, periodicals, photographs, and films. It also displays the works of renowned painters and sculptors. There are collections covering steeplechase, thoroughbred racing, shooting sports, foxhunting, and angling. The main floor of the library is open to researchers and everyone interested in quiet reading among the stacks. New members are welcome. 102 Plain Road.

Community Center and Picnic Area. Certainly among the loveliest community centers ever constructed for the purpose, when the Georgian Revival building opened in 1949 it contained a bowling alley and swimming pool. The Kennedy family held mass here while in Middleburg. Legend has it that St. Paul's Catholic Church was built to accommodate the family. The picnic tables on a small hill behind the building provide scenic respite for lunch. 300 W. Washington.

Sharon Cemetery. At the east end of Federal Street, this cemetery is a lovely public space shaded by towering conifers. Many of the family plots are sectioned by old stone walls. At the center is a memorial to Civil War unknowns; it is surrounded by eighty marked gravestones of known soldiers, many of whom died while infirmed at Middleburg after the Battle of Second Manassas.

Red Fox Inn. Established in 1728 by Joseph Chinn, the building is among the oldest surviving in the Piedmont. Long known as Mr. Chinn's Ordinary, the inn hosted the young surveyor George Washington. Later known as the Beveridge House, when it was enlarged to more than thirty rooms, the inn was used during the Civil War by Colonel John Mosby and General J.E.B Stuart. Among modern notable figures with a connection to the Red Fox, as it has been known since 1937, are President Kennedy, who held a press conference there; Jacqueline Kennedy Onassis, who stayed there regularly during the fox hunting season; and Elizabeth Taylor, a frequent guest. 2 E. Washington St.

Goose Creek Bridge. The Goose Creek Stone Bridge took the old Ashby's Gap Turnpike (Route 50) over Goose Creek just beyond its confluence with Pantherskin Creek between Middleburg and Upperville. Spanning two hundred feet with four arches, this structure is the longest of the remaining stone arch turnpike bridges in Northern Virginia. The Fauquier-Loudoun Garden Club maintains the bridge.

♨ EATING OUT, HANGING OUT

The Coach Stop. A nice little neighborhood restaurant where all the regulars meet . . . good soups and sandwiches. 9 E. Washington St.; (540) 687-5515.

Cuppa Giddy Up. Smoothies and pastries complement a praiseworthy cup. 8 E. Washington St.; (540) 687-8122.

Market Salamander. If you had to eat the same food everyday of your life, you might pick the crab cake at Salamander. Then again, it could be the hoppin' Johns or the bourbon pecan chicken salad. The macaroni and cheese wins, too. Eat inside at café tables or out on the porch. 200 W. Washington St.; (540) 687.8011.

Maxwell's. Sit outside for lunch; go inside to shoot pool upstairs or listen to acoustic music at night. 118 W. Washington St.

Mello Out. A basement carry-out featuring sandwiches and desserts—don't leave without a mini chocolate cupcake with a heap o' frosting. 2 E. Federal St.; 540-687-8635.

Middleburg Brewery & Grill. In one of Middleburg's oldest buildings, the pub features grilled specialties, its own house brews, and bottled microbrews from hither and yon. On a nice day, have a seat on the New Orleans-style porch upstairs.14 E. Federal St.; (540) 687-3454; www.middleburgbrewery.com.

Red Fox Inn. Have lunch in the historic tavern with a blazing fire—just like George Washington did. 2 E. Washington St.; (540) 687-6301.

Teddy's Pizza. New York-style pizza that Big Apple ex-pats in Washington drive out to savor. 7 E. Federal St.; (540) 687-8880.

Tirami Su. Fine Italian cuisine that has become the local favorite. 3 W. Washington St. (540) 687-8711.

Upper Crust Bakery. Wraps, sandwiches, and salads served up fresh and healthy without making a big deal of it. Pick up a bag of some of the best cookies in the area. 2 N. Pendleton St; (540) 687-5666.

✠ Distinctive Shops and Stops

Books and Crannies. Lose yourself for a while here. Features a larg selection by local writers, a room for author's readings, and a very fine children's section with colorful mural-covered walls. 15 S. Madison Street. (540) 687-6677.

The Byrne Gallery. Paintings blend seamlessly with artistic jewelry and handbags. The real surprise is the bargain-rich offerings in wearable art. 7 W. Washington St.; (540) 687-6986.

The Fun Shop. In business since 1956, the real question is: does anyone actually know how many rooms there are here? It's been called a mini department store, but that makes it sound small. Linens? Yes. Toys? Yes. Furniture, picnic baskets, clothing? Yes, yes, yes! 117 W. Washington St.; (540) 687-6590.

Home Farm. An organic grocer featuring local and naturally raised meats, dairy, and, in season, produce. Located in a stately former bank building—giving nature and food the royal treatment. Upstairs is an old-fashioned soda fountain and ice cream parlor featuring organic ice cream. It's a big "yeah." 1 E. Washington St.; (540) 687-8882.

Lou Lou. A fanciful dress and apparel shop with two other Loudoun locations and a loyal clientele. 17 S. Madison St.; (540-687-8702).

Wylie Wag. Healthy foods and just about everything else a dog could want or need; a lot of delectable doggy treats, too. 58 E. Washington St.; (540) 687-8727.

⌨ LODGING

Briar Patch. On forty-seven acres of rolling farmland, four miles east of Middleburg, with a big porch for rocking and a glass-enclosed patio. 23130 Briar Patch Lane; (703) 327–5911; www.briarpatchbandb.com.

The Goodstone Inn & Estate. A special getaway on a 265-acre country estate featuring thirteen guest rooms and suites in four individual residents, a heated outdoor pool, walking and riding trails, canoes, and bikes. Behold. 36205 Snake Hill Rd.; (540) 687-4645; www.goodstone.com.

Middleburg Country Inn. At once elegant and cozy, with one of the more comforting dining rooms you'll ever encounter. Ice cream is always available to guests, as is a slice of lemon cake made from a family recipe. In downtown Middleburg. 209 E. Washington St.; (540) 687-6082; www.middleburgcountryinn.com.

Red Fox Inn. To many people, the Red Fox is synonymous with Middleburg. It's hosted political leaders and the well known since its founding in 1728. 2 E. Washington St.; (540) 687-6301; www.redfox.com.

———

From Middleburg, travel west on Route 50 through the village of Upperville and over the Blue Ridge into Clarke County. A mile after crossing the Shenandoah River, turn right onto Road 723 toward Millwood (if you miss the turn, go another half mile and turn right onto Route 255). Merge onto Route 255 just before entering the village.

Millwood

Situated on a quiet country road, Millwood is a tiny settlement that was once adjacent to the 5,500-acre plantation owned by Nathanial Burwell. Grandson of Robert "King" Carter, the patriarch of a Virginia founding family, Burwell commanded a militia in Washington's army at Yorktown. This plantation in the Shenandoah Valley was part of his inheritance. He and his local partner, Daniel Morgan, established the mill here in 1782. In the 1790s, Burwell constructed Carter Hall, one of the grandest manor homes in Virginia.

The village consists of the mill, post office, a dozen houses, and a few commercial buildings. The centerpiece of the town is **Locke Store**, which has been operating as a store since 1836. Its latest rendition is as a gourmet country store offering a rotating menu of sandwiches, salads, specialty foods, and deli dishes—all with an emphasis on local ingredients. Each evening there are one or two take-out entrees.

Burwell-Morgan Mill. Built to serve the booming population of the Shenandoah Valley, the mill employs an internal waterwheel twenty feet in diameter. A double set of wooden gears turns two pairs of grindstones, one for wheat and one for corn. No doubt its operation became routine for the men who worked there through nearly two centuries, but it's a pretty extraordinary site for us. The mill is open Thursday through Sunday and operates milling demonstrations on Saturdays. In spring and autumn, Art at the Mill presents hundreds of paintings for sale at the mill. There are picnic grounds by the tailrace. The mill is operated by Clarke County Historical Society; (540) 837-1799; www.clarkehistory.org.

Christ Church. Driving north on Route 255, a half mile from the mill is Christ Episcopal Church, a striking stone chapel built on land donated by Nathaniel Burwell. It's a peaceful place for a rest.

Red Schoolhouse Antiques. This 1850s building was a girls' school, then later the Blue Ridge Day School, which operated here

Burwell-Morgan Mill.
Photo: Steven L. Spring

until 1989. There are six antique dealers exhibiting furnishing, prints, household items, and art in the ten-room shop.

———

Continuing north on Route 255, at the junction with Route 340 is Old Chapel, which predates Christ Church and is part of the same parish, founded in 1738. Old Chapel was built in 1790 with financial support from Nathaniel Burwell, who is buried here in the church cemetery. Governor Edmund Radford also is buried here. Lord Fairfax worshipped here, while living in nearby White Post.

Turn right onto Route 340 and continue three miles into Berryville.

Berryville. Berryville was chartered in 1798 at the site of a crossroads inn, on the broad Shenandoah Valley west of the Blue Ridge. The names on the area's early land patents reflect those of the Tidewater and Piedmont, names such Washington and Carter. Berryville is the county seat and the big town of Clarke County, containing a couple of blocks of handsome brick offices, the courthouse, and impressive residences set back from the street. The old courthouse on North Church Street illustrates the Jefferson influence on public buildings that by 1838 was taking hold throughout the region.

South Church Street is a quiet avenue of dignified residences inviting a leisurely afternoon stroll. In the lovely **Rose Hill Park** on East Main Street, there are free concerts each Friday in the warm months. Across from the park is the **Clarke County Historical Society and Museum**, which contains a small collection of artifacts offering tall tales. One involves a clock, formerly on a plantation nearby. It seems a repairman offered to service all the clocks on the premises in exchange for room and board. He was ordered from the premises for urging the enslaved servants to flee. The repairman was John Brown.

Next to the museum is **Gold Leaf**, a gift store established in the old **Coiner Store**, which operated for a hundred years beginning in 1896. The pulley-system cash carrier is still there. Using wood cups and a network of metal wires strung from the ceiling, clerks zipped cash payments from any location in the store to the cashier in the loft. Change was returned in the same cup. Ask for a demonstration.

Stop in the **Berryville Old Book Shop** for some browse time. It's a classic case of a booklover whose collection has outgrown his home—big enough to lose yourself but small enough that the proprietor can pinpoint the object of your search and name a half dozen related titles. Among the notable collections are those on Virginia history, U.S. politics and government, drama and performing arts, and natural history. The children's room is a winner.

Berryville Newsstand, one of the oldest businesses in town, has morphed into the **Daily Grind**, a coffee shop with a newsstand attached—it's a snug place to examine your take from the bookshop. If you arrive in the morning, go for the pastries at **Bon Matin** bakery; head to **Jane's** for lunch. Also on Main Street are a tavern, a Mexican cantina, and a pizza place. A few blocks away on West Main is the **Battletown Inn**. Built in 1809, this Federal-style structure is among the oldest in town. The historic Inn, which underwent extensive restoration in 2005, offers lodging and dining.

———

Drive east on Route 7 toward the Blue Ridge. Cross the Shenandoah River and climb the mountain. For extraordinary views of the Shenandoah Valley, stop at Bears Den at the top of the ridge. There are two ways to access the rocks with the great views, one involves a fifteen-minute hike on the Appalachian Trail; it departs from the commuter lot at the crest on Route 7. The other way up is to turn right on Blueridge Mountain Road and drive a half mile. Turn right into Bears Den Trail Center, a hikers' hostel set in a beautiful stone cottage. Drive up the gravel lane to the trailhead. From the trailhead, the rocks are only a five-minute hike away. Whenever you see a magazine cover shot of the Northern Shenandoah Valley, chances are it was taken here. If the Bears Den store is open, you can stop in for trail snacks.

———

Back at Route 7, turn right to descend the mountain. On the descent, pass the north end of Snickersville Turnpike, which leads downhill to the village of Bluemont. Down on the Piedmont is Round Hill, a historic village where the Round Hill Arts Center hosts bluegrass and arts classes. To visit Purcellville for dinner, turn right onto Business Route 7.

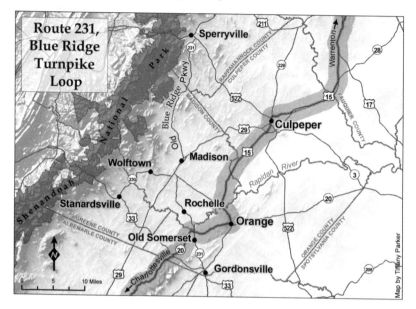

Map by Tiffany Parker

8. Route 231, Blue Ridge Turnpike Loop

Highlights: Travel the western edge of the Piedmont in Orange and Madison counties on the historic Blue Ridge Turnpike, one of the most scenic drives of the Appalachian Mountains.

Distance: About 60 miles, with return via Culpeper.

From Orange, travel south on Route 15 toward Gordonsville. There are long views of Orange County, but this is truly Madison Country. Land in the vicinity was part of the Madison family's Montpelier patent of 1723. More than a hundred years after the family's arrival here, estates and plantations were still being created from the original holding. Mayhurst, built in the 1850s, now a B&B, was the home of John Willis, great grandnephew of James Madison.

Gordonsville, named for Nathaniel Gordon, who kept an inn here in the late eighteenth century. Thomas Jefferson, Major General the Marquis de Lafayette, and other notable figures of early America were guests at the tavern. The village grew rapidly with the arrival of two railroads in the 1840s and early 1850s. Gordonsville also was at the crossroads of two major turnpikes.

The Civil War was the first war to rely on railroad to transport supplies and soldiers. As a transportation hub served by rail and road, Gordonsville became strategically important to the Confederate Army. In 1862, Stonewall Jackson had his headquarters at the old Gordon Tavern for several days. The Gordonsville Receiving Hospital, which occupied the stylish Exchange Hotel, treated and cared for more than seventy thousand soldiers. The former hotel–hospital is now the **Exchange Hotel Civil War Museum**, an essential stop on The Journey Through Hallowed Ground.

———

Leaving Gordonsville, travel north on route 231, the old Blue Ridge Parkway through scenic rolling hills with mountain views and glimpses of historic estates (see Orange County, Tours, for information on guided history tours).

At the junction with Route 20 is Old Somerset. The charming chapel is Somerset Christian Church. Built circa 1857, its Italianate bracketed cornice and porch are a departure from the Gothic and Greek Revival styles of most nineteenth-century Virginia country churches. The structure is virtually unaltered from its original appearance; the interior retains its original furnishings, including its pews. From here, look south, back toward Gordonsville, for an open view of Somerset House, home of Thomas Macon and Sarah Catlett Madison Macon, sister of President Madison.

North of Route 20, cross the Rapidan River into Madison County. The views along the Blue Ridge Turnpike become more open and expansive. To the west are nearly continuous imposing views of the mountains. The Battle of Jack's Shop was fought in and around the crossroads village of Rochelle. There is a roadside Civil War Trails marker overlooking a farm field a short distance north of the settlement. In this afternoon battle on September 22, 1863, J.E.B. Stuart was ambushed during retreat and almost captured by Union cavalry under Kilpatrick and John Buford. The countryside today looks much the way it did at the time of the battle. Most of the homes dotting the old turnpike were present then.

At the junction with Route 230, you can continue north toward Madison or enjoy an interlude of picnicking and a hike along the Rapidan River in Shenandoah National Park. For this side trip, turn left on Route 230 and follow the route west across Route 29 to Wolftown (for a short cut, instead of turning left onto 230, turn left onto Shelby Road, Route 662, which will rejoin Route 230). In Wolftown, stop at the Wolftown Mercantile Country Store for a picnic lunch—fried chicken and a couple of sides for about five bucks.

From the Wolftown store, follow Route 662 six miles through striking scenery past the former village of Graves Mill, which was wiped out in the flood of 1995. At the Staunton River trailhead in Shenandoah National Park, you can find a picnic spot at the trailhead, then take an easy stroll upstream to little pools and sunny boulders. The trail leads four miles up to Bear Rock Church, alternately known as Bear Church Rock, where there are incredible views of the Rapidan valley. It's a strenuous three-hour round trip trek, only for the hearty (and definitely not for little kids), but the rewards are legend.

Back on the Journey, Route 231 leads into Madison, the county seat. The county courthouse, completed in 1830, is an architectural marvel of federal-style craftsmanship. The museum at the Madison **Arcade Building** exhibits artifacts and interprets local history. President and Mrs. Hoover had ties to Madison. Hoover personally financed the construction of Camp Hoover, a mountain retreat meant for U.S. presidents and their advisers, not far from here. You can visit the retreat from Skyline Drive in Shenandoah National Park.

There are three restaurants on Main Street, ranging from pizza to a family restaurant to the upscale **Madison Inn**. They are all within a few steps of one another There also is a lunch counter at **Madison Pharmacy**, where you can have a sandwich and a fountain soda.

Route 231 north from Madison to Sperryville is surely among the most beautiful scenic drives in America. Mile after mile of pasture along the road creates open views of the mountains in Shenandoah National Park. In Banco, the Old Blue Ridge Turnpike breaks left to disappear into the mountains, where it now ends at the Rose River. You can keep traveling the Blue Ridge Turnpike on foot, up and over the mountain. On the road to Sperryville, there are a couple of roadside stores where you can stop for snacks. Along the way, there also are trailheads into the national park—most notable is the one at Old Rag Mountain.

Route 231 ends at Route 522, just east of Sperryville. To complete this scenic loop via Culpeper, turn right. To return via Skyline Drive, turn left and follow the signs. At Skyline Drive, you will travel south to Route 33, which leads east through the historic town of Standardsville en route to Orange. Either way, a stop in the one-street town of Sperryville is in order. Here, you'll find a fine little bookstore, an old-fashioned grocery, a couple galleries, and a few restaurants.

Photo: CMW

—About The Journey Through Hallowed Ground Partnership—

*T*he Journey Through Hallowed Ground Partnership is a nonprofit organization dedicated to raising national awareness of the unparalleled history in the region, which generally follows the Old Carolina Road (Rt. 15/231) from Gettysburg, through Maryland, to Monticello in Albemarle County, VA. From its communities, farms, businesses, and heritage sites, we have an opportunity to celebrate and preserve this vital fabric of America, which stands today in the historic, scenic and natural beauty of this region. The Journey Through Hallowed Ground is dedicated to encouraging both Americans and world visitors to **Take the Journey**™ to appreciate, respect, and experience this cultural landscape that makes it uniquely American.

We are doing this by:

- Building a strong network of local, regional, and national partners to develop a common vision for the conservation and enhancement of the scenic, historic, recreational, cultural, and natural characteristics of the region.
- Developing educational programs for students and teachers within the region as well as across the country so that they can learn about the stories of the ordinary people who did extraordinary things to shape this nation.

- Helping national, state and regional parks, historic downtown communities, museums, and heritage sites promote the region, showcasing that while this is *Where America Happened*, it's also where it continues to happen every day.

- Working in partnership with local, state, and national officials to create a National Scenic Byway and a National Heritage Area to sustain and strengthen our economy, heritage and quality of life in this region.

For more information on how you can become involved, please visit www.HallowedGround.org.

Answers to The Journey Through Hallowed Ground's Historical Quiz (opposite page):
(From left to right)
Line 1: Clara Barton, President Theodore Roosevelt
Line 2: President Dwight D. Eisenhower, "Bloody Ban" Banastre Tarleton, Frederick Douglass
Line 3: John Brown, President Thomas Jefferson

Who Are These Hallowed Faces?!

The Journey Through Hallowed Ground invites you to take this historical quiz!

Hint: She was the "Angel of the Battlefield" at Antietam.

"HEAVENLY!"

"BULLY!"

Hint: His rustic retreat, "Pine Knott" is near Keene, Va.

"I LIKE IT!"

Hint: His farm at Gettysburg has a putting green!

Hint: This British Dragoon chased Virginia's Governor and Legislature up a mountain in Albemarle County, Virginia.

"REVOLUTIONARY"

Hint: A school in Leesburg, Va named for him was the first built and paid for by African-Americans

"AT LAST!"

Hint: His bloody insurrection at Harper's Ferry helped ignite the Civil War.

"GLORY!"

"STUPENDOUS!"

Hint: His home near Charlottesville has an Italian name.

Index

Acacia Fusion Bistro, 37
Accentuates, 40
Ace Books & Antiques, 115
Adams, John Quincy, 64, 75
Adams County, 1–3, 5, 13, 174–175, 184–189.
    See also specific sites; specific towns
Adams County Winery, 20–21, 188
African American heritage, 54, 176–185
    Adams and Frederick Counties, 12, 36,
        184–185
    Albemarle and Orange Counties, 150, 176–
        178
    Fauquier County, 178–180
    Harpers Ferry, 182–184, 198
    Loudoun County, xiv, 60, 62, 76, 179–182,
        200
Afro-American Historical Association of
    Fauquier County, 178–180
Ala Heart Café, 113
Albemarle Charlottesville Historical Society,
    154, 161
Albemarle County, 125–126, 145–164, 168–172,
    176–177. *See also specific sites; specific
    towns*
Albemarle County Courthouse, 155
Aldie, battle of, 207
Aldie Mill Historic District, 23, 56, 76–77, 207
Amber Coast, 40
American Revolution, xvii, 54, 90, 108, 168, 203,
    213
Another Dimension, 115
Antietam, battle of, 43–44, 207
Antiques, etc., 196
A.P. Hill Boyhood Home, 89, 110
Appalachian Mountains, 187, 218
Appalachian Trail, 3, 45, 202, 203, 216
Arcade Building, 220
Art Center in Orange, 137
Art Upstairs, 158
Artworks, 16
Ash Lawn-Highland, 123, 145–147, 152, 160,
    167, 168
Avenue Restaurant, 13
Averell, William, 105–106
Avocado, 158

B&O Railroad, 5, 196
Baby Jim's Snack Bar, 113
Ballard, Garland, 131

Ballard-Marshall House, 131
Ball's Bluff Battlefield Regional Park, 53, 62–
    63
Ball's Bluff National Cemetery, 62–63
Banco, 221
Banshee Reeks, 53, 74–75
Barbour, James, 140, 143, 171
Barboursville, 123, 140, 142–144, 171–172
Barboursville Vineyards, 140, 143, 171
Barn Swallow, 158
Battle That Saved Washington, 4, 34–35
Battlefield Bed & Breakfast, 17
battles and battle fields, Civil War
    Adams County, 2–3, 5–6, 8–13, 15, 20–23,
        105, 175
    Culpeper County, 89–90, 92, 104–108,
        111–112, 119–120
    Frederick County, 4, 34–35, 43–45, 201–
        204, 207
    Loudoun County, 53, 62–63, 207
    Madison County, 219
    Orange County, 134, 144, 172–173
    Prince William County, 43, 84–86, 98, 178,
        209
Battletown Inn, 216
Bead Shoppe, 99–100
Beans and Bagels, 37
Beans in the Belfry, 197
Bear Rock Church, 220
Beatty-Cramer House, 33–34
Beekeepers Cottage, 57
Bella-Mia's Italian American Deli, 113
Belmont Farms Distillery, 118
Berkley Gallery, 100
Berryville, 215–216
Berryville Newsstand, 216
Berryville Old Book Shop, 216
Berrywine Plantation/Linganore Winecellars,
    45–46
bicycling, 21, 47, 103, 104, 125
Bizou Diner, 157
Black Horse Inn, 101
Black Shutter Antique Center, 69
Black Voices, 183
Blue Parrot Bistro, 15
Blue Ridge Center for Environmental
    Stewardship, 82, 198
Blue Ridge Grill, 66
Blue Ridge Mountains, xvii, 2, 30, 118–119, 141

Blue Ridge Turnpike, 218–221
Blue Whale Used & Rare Books, 158
Bluegrass in Lucketts, 57
Bon Matin Bakery, 216
Book Cellar, 16, 158–159
Book Crossing, 197
Books and Crannies, 211
Boone, Daniel, 155
Boyds Bear Country, 18–19
Brafferton Inn, 18
Brandy Station Battlefield, 89, 90, 106–107
Breaux Vineyards, 79, 199
Brewer's Alley Restaurant and Brewery, 37
Briar Patch, 212
Brick House Inn, 18
Broad Run Baptist Church, 89
Brossman's Orchard, 80–81
Brown, John, 182, 198, 215
Bruner, Elias, 36–37
Brunswick, 47, 195–197
Brunswick Railroad Museum, 195–196
Buckland, 53, 86–87
Buckland Races, 86, 89–90
Buford, John, 219
Burgandine House, 110–111
Burkittsville, 44–45, 203
Burnley Vineyards, 140
Burwell, Nathaniel, 213, 215
Burwell-Morgan Mill, 213–214
Byrne Gallery, The, 211
B'z Barbecue, 67

C&O Canal, 44, 47, 49, 58–59, 77, 195–196, 198
C&O Canal National Historical Park, 4–5, 58–59, 196
Café Cubana Coffee, 157
Calhoun, Tom, 115
Calhoun's Country Hams, 115
Cameleer, 115
Cameron Street Coffee, 113
Camp David, 28–29, 166, 174, 192
Camp David Museum, 28, 174, 192
Camp Hoover, 220
Candy Stick Restaurant, 39, 191
Carriage House Inn, 25
Carroll, Charles, 3, 42
Carroll Creek, 32
Carrollton House, 42
Carter, George, 73–74
Carter, Robert "King," 73–74, 213, 215
Cascade Inn, 28
Cashtown Inn, 15, 188
Castaway Company, 115
Catoctin Furnace, 1, 26–27, 192, 193
Catoctin Inn, 41–42
Catoctin Mountain Orchard, 26, 29, 46
Catoctin Mountain Park, 192
Catoctin Mountains, 3, 26–27, 30, 54, 174, 190–193

Catoctin Pottery, 46
Catoctin Wildlife Preserve, 29
Cedar Mountain Battlefield, 89, 92, 119–120
cemeteries
  Adams County, 12, 174, 175, 184
  Culpeper and Fauquier Counties, 89, 98, 111
  Loudoun County, 62–63, 209
Chancellorsville, battle of, 144
Charlottesville, 2, 123, 125–126, 153–163
Charlottesville Courthouse, 125
Charlottesville Ice Park, 160
Chateau du Reaux, 115
Chinn, Joseph, 209
Christ Episcopal Church, 213
Christine Fox, 100
Chronicle of the Horse (sculpture), 208
Chubby's Southern Style Barbecue, 25
Church of Our Savior, 74
Civil Rights Movement, 60, 63–64, 180, 182–184
Civil War, xvii–xviii, 4, 5. *See also specific battles*
  Adams and Frederick counties, 184–185, 202–204
  cemeteries, 12, 62–63, 89, 98, 111, 174–175, 184, 209
  Fauquier and Culpeper counties, 90, 104–107, 108, 119–120
  Harpers Ferry, 182
  hospitals and medicine, 35–36, 50, 76
  Loudoun and Prince William counties, 54–56, 76, 84–86, 182, 194–195, 207–209
  Madison and Orange counties, 134, 144, 173, 219
  trails and transportation operations, 48–50, 59
Civil War Museum at the Exchange Hotel, 144
Claire's at the Depot, 98
Clarke County, 212–217
Clarke County Historical Society and Museum, 215
Classic Touch Consigned Furniture, 137
Clay, Henry, 96
Clifton, 160
C.M. Crockett Park, 103
Coach Stop, 210
Cobean, Alexander, 13
Cochran, William, 32
Coffee Bean, 66
Coiner Store, 215–216
College of William and Mary, 147
Cooling Springs Farm, 48
Copper Kettle Soup Bar, 114
Corner, The, 154
Country Gardens, 144
Court Square, 155, 160
Court Square Tavern, 157
Cozy Inn and Restaurant, 28–29, 174, 192
Crampton's Gap, battle of, 203, 204

Crème de la Crème, 70
Crooked Run Orchard, 81
Culpeper (town), 89, 107–119, 167, 173. *See also*
    specific sites
Culpeper County, 90–92, 103, 107–120. *See also*
    Culpeper (town); *specific sites*
Culpeper Courthouse, battle of, 112
Culpeper Minutemen, 108
Culpeper National Cemetery, 89, 111
Culpeper Railroad Depot, 112
Cunningham Falls State Park, 26–27, 29, 30, 47,
    191, 193
Cuppa Giddy Up, 210
Custer, George, 92, 112

Daedalus Books, 158–159
Dahlgren, Madeleine, 44, 202
Dahlgren Chapel, 44, 202
Daily Grind, 216
Dancing Bear Toys and Gifts, 40
Dave's Deli and Café, 134–135
David Wills House, 13, 174–175
Davis, Westmoreland, 60, 65
Dean, Jennie, 178
Dee Dee's Family Restaurant, 113
Delaplaine Visual Arts Education Center, 40
Designs by Teresa, 100
Dinsmore, James, 160
Dinsmore House, 160
Dobbin House, 14–15, 185
Dodona Manor, 53, 60, 63
Douglas, Frederick, 178, 198
Downtown Saloon, 66
Du Bois, W.E.B., 183, 198
duPont Scott, Marion, 130

Early, Jubal, 34–35, 49
Earthly Paradise, 98
Eiffel Tower Café, 66
Eisenhower, Dwight D. and Mamie, 8, 17, 22,
    174, 175
Eisenhower National Historic Site, xvii, 8–9,
    175
Ekster Antiques & Uniques, 70
El Vaquero West, 135
Elk Run Vineyards, 46
Emmanuel Episcopal Church, 119
Emmitsburg, 1, 3, 23–26
Ernie's Texas Lunch, 15
Eunice's Restaurant, 39
Everedy Square/Shab Row, 40
Exchange Hotel Civil War Museum, 219

Fabbioli, Doug, 118
Fairfax, Thomas, Lord, 215
Fairfield, 21–22, 187
Fairfield Inn, 185
Farmer John's Wayside Stand, 81–82
Farnsworth House, 15, 19, 185

Fauquier County, 89–106, 178–180. *See also*
    specific sites; specific towns
Fauquier County Courthouse, 89, 94–95
Fauquier County Library, 95–96
Felini's #9, 157
Firestone's Restaurant and Bar, 38
Fluvanna Courthouse Historic District, 163
Food for Thought, 116
Foti's, 113–114
Fountain Hall B&B, 117
Frederick (town), xviii, 1, 3–4, 30–48. *See also*
    specific sites
Frederick County, 1–2, 3–5, 34, 174, 190–193,
    195–198, 201–204. *See also specific*
    sites; specific towns
Frederick Municipal Forest, 46–47
French and Indian War, xvii, 17, 64, 93, 108
Frenchman's Corner, 116
Frost Café, 114
Fun Shop, 211

Gallery 30, 16
Gallery 222, 70
Galletta's Pasta & Italian Specialties, 66
Gambrill, James, 47
Gambrill State Park, 47, 191
Gaslight Inn, 18
Gathland State Park, 45, 203–204
German immigrants, 1–3, 37, 54, 103
Gettysburg (town), xviii, 1–22, 174–175, 184–
    185
Gettysburg Address, 12, 167, 174, 175
Gettysburg College, 175
Gettysburg National Battlefield and Military
    Park, 2–3, 5–6, 8–13, 15, 20–23,
    105, 175
ghost tours, 19, 42, 72
Gilbert's Corner, 75
Gilmore, George, 177
Gilmore Cabin, 177–178
Gleedsville Gallery, 70
Gold Leaf, 215–216
Goodstone Inn & Estate, 212
Goose Creek Bridge, 209
Gordon, Nathaniel, 144, 218
Gordonsville, 123, 142, 144–145, 218–219
Graffiti House Museum, 89, 106–107
Grant, Ulysses, 95, 134, 173
Graves Mill, 220
Gravity Lounge, 157
Great Bridge, battle of, 108
Great Country Farms, 82
Greenock House Inn, 138
Grotto of Lourdes, 1, 23, 24–25

Hamilton, 78, 205–206
Hansen, Brad, 118
Hansen, Susan, 46
Hanson, John, 32
Happy Garden Chinese Restaurant, 135

Hare Hill, 137
Harpers Ferry National Historical Park, 182–184, 198
Harrison, Benjamin, 155
Hatten Ferry, 161
Haymarket, 84
Hazel River Inn, 114, 117
Hebron Lutheran Church, 141
Hemp Meats, 201
Henry, Patrick, 22, 155
Hidden Brook Winery, 58
Highland Farm Inn, 101–102
highlands tour, 186–189
Hill, A.P., 15, 111, 186, 188
Hill, E.B., 111
Hill House Bed & Breakfast, 41
Hill Mansion, 111–112
Hillsborough Winery, 199
Historical Society of Frederick County, 34
Hoban, James, 75
Holladay House, 128, 138
Hollerstown Hill, 41
Home Farm, 211
Homefront 40's, 16
Homespun, 144
Hooker, Joseph, 107
Hoover, Herbert, 140, 220
Horse Country Saddlery, 100
Horton Vineyards, 140
hot air balloon rides, 161
Houston, Charles, 60, 63–64, 180

Imagine That, 72
Inn at Buckeystown, 42
Inn at Court Square, 160
Inn at Kelly's Ford, 102
Inn at Meander Plantation, 126, 135–136, 139
Inn on Poplar Hill, 138
Irish immigrants, 1–3, 54, 75
Iroquois Indians, xvii, 54
It's About Thyme, 114

Jack's Shop, battle of, 219
Jackson, Andrew, 96
Jackson, Thomas (Stonewall), 85, 92, 119–120, 155, 219
Jackson Park, 155
Jacqueline Kennedy Pavilion, 208
James Gettys Hotel, 18
James Madison Museum, 132–133
Janal Leather, 116
Jane's, 216
Janney, Amos, 200
Jefferson (town), 201
Jefferson, Thomas, 131, 138, 143, 145, 146
    Lewis and Clark Expedition, 125–126
    Monticello, 147–150, 168
    places visited by, 144, 155, 198, 218
    University of Virginia, 153, 156, 171
Jefferson Pastry Shoppe, 201

Jefferson Vineyards, 161
Jennie Dean Memorial, 178
Jimmie's Market, 98
John Brown Museum, 182
John Mosby House, 89, 95
Johnson, Thomas, 3, 30, 36
Jouett, Jack, 155
Journey Through Hallowed Ground, described, xvii–xx, 153, 165–167, 176
Journey Through Hallowed Ground Partnership, xix–xx, 223–224
J.S. Mosby Antiques and Artifacts, 137
Just Jennifer, 16–17

Kelly's Ford Battlefield, 89, 90, 105–106
Kemper Park, 162
Kennedy, Jacqueline, 208, 209
Kennedy, John F., 209
Key, Francis Scott, 32
Kilpatrick, Hugh Judson, 219
King Family Vineyards, 161
Kings Pizza, 197
Kluge-Ruhe, 158
Knights of the Golden Horseshoe, 126
Kountry Kitchen, 28

La Cucina, 157
Lafayette, Marquis de, 64, 75, 96, 144, 218
Lamar House, 202
Lander Lock House, 195
Layngs Flower Farm, 82
Le Savon, 40
Lee, Fitzhugh, 105–107
Lee, Richard Henry, 90, 94, 155
Lee, Robert E., 22, 35, 43, 85, 105, 111, 128, 134, 173
Lee Park, 155
Leesburg, xviii, 23, 54–56, 59–72, 180–181
Leesburg African American Heritage Trail, 180–182
Leesburg Antiques Emporium, 70
Leesburg Colonial Inn, 71
Leesburg Restaurant, 67
Leesburg Vintner, 70–71
Lewis, Abraham, 125
Lewis, Meriwether, 125–126, 198
Lewis and Clark Expedition, 125–126
Library Used Book Store, 137
Lightfoot Restaurant, 67
Lincoln (town), 206
Lincoln, Abraham, 12, 13, 96, 167, 174, 175
Lincoln Cemetery, 12, 184
Lincoln Square, 7, 174–175
Linganore Winecellars, 45–46
Little Apple Pastry Shop, 77
Little River Inn, 77
Little River Turnpike, 76–77
Locke Store, 213
Loew Vineyards, 46
Longstreet, James, 207

Lord Nelson's Nature Store and Gallery, 17
Lost Creek Winery, 58
Lou Lou, 211
Loudoun County, 53–83, 173, 179–182,
    194–195, 200, 205–212. *See also*
    specific sites; specific towns
Loudoun Courthouse, 63–64, 179–180
Loudoun Museum, 64
Loy's Station Covered Bridge Park, 29, 193
Lucio, 114
Lucketts, 53, 57–59, 194
Lutheran Theological Seminary, 7

Macon, Sarah Catlett Madison, 143, 219
Macon, Thomas, 143, 219
Madison (town), 141, 142, 220
Madison, Francis, 127
Madison, James, 128, 146
    Montpelier, 130–132, 172
    places visited by, 125, 155
    relatives of, 138, 142
Madison, William, 127
Madison County, 123–125, 126–127, 139, 141,
    219–220. *See also specific sites; specific*
    towns
Madison Inn Restaurant, 141, 220
Madison Pharmacy, 220
Madison Tea Room, 98
Madison-Barboursville Historic District, 142
Main Street Bistro, 99
Majestic Theater, 7, 17
Mama's, 144
Manassas (town), 83, 86, 178
Manassas, battles of, 43, 84–86, 98, 178, 209
Manassas Battlefield Military Park, 84–86, 209
Manassas Industrial School, 178
Mario's Pizza and Pasta Buffet, 135
Market Salamander, 210
Market Station, 71
Market Street Café, 38
Market Street Coffee, 67
Marshall, Fielding Lewis, 131
Marshall, George C., 60, 63
Marshall, John, 90, 93, 94–95, 100, 131
Marshall Plan, 63
Marta von Dettingen, 100
Maryland Ensemble Theater, 31, 41
Maxwell's, 210
Mayhurst Inn, 138, 218
McClellan, George, 96, 207
McGuffey Art Center, 158
McGuire Fine Art, 41
Meade, George, 105
Mellow Out, 210
Melrose Antiques, 137
Mercer, Charles Fenton, 76–77
Meriwether, Nicholas, 125
Micheaux State Forest, 3, 21–22
Michie Tavern, 151–152
Middleburg, 78, 207–212

Middleburg Brewery & Grill, 210
Middleburg Country Inn, 212
Middletown, 44–45, 202
Mighty Midget, 67
Millwood, 213–215
Molly's Irish Pub, 99
Mom's Apple Pie Bakery, 68, 101
Monocacy Aqueduct, 44
Monocacy National Battlefield, 4, 34–35
Monroe, James
    Ash Lawn-Highland, 145–147, 168
    Oak Hill, 75, 173
    places visited by, 64, 96, 125, 155
Monroe Doctrine, 55, 75, 146, 173
Montalto, 151
Monticello, 123–124, 126, 147–150, 161–162,
    168, 176–177
Monticello Hotel Partners, 159
Montpelier, 123, 128, 130–132, 172, 177–178,
    218
Morgan, Daniel, 213
Morven Park, 53, 59, 60, 64–65
Mosby, John Singleton, xiii, 49, 54, 76, 93, 95,
    98, 209
Mosby Heritage Area, 54
Mosby's Rangers, 49, 54, 76, 95, 127
Mount Zion Church, 53, 76
Mountain Gap School, 74
Mountain Gate, 28
Mountain Run Lake Park, 118–119
Mudhouse Coffee, 157
Mulberry Row, 176–177
Muse, The, 41
Museum of Culpeper History, 112
My Wits End Antiques, 56

National Fallen Firefighters Memorial, 23, 25
National Museum of Civil War Medicine,
    35–36
National Shrine of Elizabeth Ann Seton,
    23–24
National Sporting Library, 208
Natural Marketplace, 99
Natural Mercantile, 205
Neilson, John, 160
Nesbitt, Mark, 19
New Dominion Book Shop, 158–159
New Market, 48
New Oxford, 22
Niagara Movement, 183–184
Nichols, Frederick, 143
Nichols Galleries, 143
Norris House Inn, 72
Not The Same Old Grind and Orange Roasters,
    135

Oak Hill, 53, 55, 75, 146, 173
Oakencroft Vineyard & Winery, 162
Oakleys' Gently Used Books, 158–159
Oatlands Historic District, 53, 55, 72–74

Old Carolina Road, xvii, 5, 51, 54–56, 72, 76, 84. *See also* U.S. Route 15
Old Chapel Church, 215
Old House Vineyards, 118
Old Jail Museum, 89, 90, 95–96
Old Lucketts School, 57
Old Lucketts Store, 57
Old Rag Mountain, 141–142, 221
Old Somerset, 142, 219
Old Somerset Gallery, 144
Old Stone Jail Museum, 163
Old Town Manassas, 86
Onassis, Jacqueline Kennedy, 208, 209
Orange, Town of, 127–140
Orange and Alexandria Line, 134
Orange County, 123, 125–140, 142–145, 172–173, 177–178, 218–219. *See also specific sites; specific towns*
Orange County Courthouse, 133
Orange Historical Society, 134
Orange Railway Station, 134
Orchard Market, 20
orchards tour, 186–189
O'Rourke's, 16
Ott House Pub, 25
Oxo, 157

Paisley, Bob, 57
Paladio Restaurant, 143
Palms, The, 26
Palmyra, 163
Patowmack Farm, 56
Payne, William H.F., 93
Pearmund Cellars, 102
Pelham, John, 106
Petite Dekor, 71
Petoile, 157
Philomont, 207
Picket, Martin, 93
pick-your-own fruit, 26, 29, 46, 80–81, 82
Piedmont Episcopal Church, 141
Pine Grove Furnace State Park, 21–22
Pine Knot Cabin, 168, 170–171
Point of Rocks, 1, 48–53, 56, 194–195
Potomac Heritage Trail, 82
Potomac River, 2, 4–5, 53, 55–56, 58–59, 82, 194–200
Powell, Ambrose, 110
presidential tour, 166–175
Prince Michel Vineyards, 118
Prince William County, 83–87, 178. *See also specific sites; specific towns*
Proof Artisan Bakery, 38
Prospect Hill, 127
Pub, The, 114
Puccio's New York Deli, 68
Purcellville, 72, 78

Quakers, xiv–xv, 181–182, 200, 206

Radford, Edmund, 215
Ragged Edge Coffee House, 16
Ragged Mountain Natural Area, 162–163
railroads, scenic, 20, 43
Randolph, Thomas Mann, Jr., 160
Rapidan Historic District, 119
Rapidan River, 117, 119, 123, 125, 127, 219–220
Rappahannock, battles of, 89, 104–107, 111
Rappahannock River, 90, 103–105, 117
Rappahannock Station Battlefield, 89, 105
Read It Again Sam, 158–159
Really Great Finds, 57
Red Fox Inn, 209, 210, 212
Red Rock Wilderness Overlook, 83
Red Schoolhouse Antiques, 214–215
Redman, Don, 183
Remington, 103, 104, 105
Remington Bicycle Trails, 103
Renee's Gourmet to Go, 99
Reno, Jesse, 203
Residence, The, 127
Restaurant Pomme, 145
Rivanna Trails, 162
Robert H. Smith International Center for Jefferson Studies, 168
Rochelle, 219
Roddy Covered Bridge, 1, 26, 29
Roger Brooke Taney House, 36
Rogers Ford Farm Winery, 102
Roosevelt, Edith, 170
Roosevelt, Franklin Delano, 174, 192
Roosevelt, Theodore, 170–171
Rose Hill Manor, 1, 30, 36
Rose Hill Park, 215
Rouge, 71
Round Barn, 21, 189
Round Hill, 217
Route 231, xx, 219–221
Rupp House History Center, 12
Rust Sanctuary, 83

Sach's Bridge, 19–20, 187
Sage Moon, 158
Sara Schneidman Gallery, 116
Schifferstadt Architectural Museum, 36–37
Scots-Irish immigrants, 1, 3, 54, 75
Second Street Gallery, 158
Seton, Elizabeth Ann, 23–24
Shab Row, 40
Shadwell, 145, 151
Sharon Cemetery, 209
Shelf Life, 101
Shenandoah National Park, 140–141, 163, 220–221
Shenandoah River, 184, 198
Shenandoah Valley, 55, 84, 107, 126, 213–217
Short Hill, 80, 199
Shrine to Elizabeth Ann Seton, 1
Shriver House Museum, 13

Silk Mill Grille, 135
601 Deli, 144
Sleepy Hollow Farm, 139
Smith, William (Extra Billy), 93
Smokey Joe's Café, 99
Soldiers National Cemetery, 12, 174, 175
Somerset Christian Church, 142, 219
Somerset House, 142, 219
Sons of Good Will, 12, 184
South Mountain, 2, 8–9, 22, 44, 46, 188, 201–204
South Mountain Inn, 44, 202–203
South Mountain State Battlefield, 44–45, 201–204
South Street Brewery, 158
South Street Under, 68
Sparks Bistro, 135
Sparks Building, 128
Sperryville, 221
Spotswood, Alexander, 117, 126
St. Paul's Church, 50
Stavarus Pizza, 26
steeplechase racing, 65, 118, 208
Stonewall Jackson, 85, 92, 119–120, 155, 219
Storer College Niagara Exhibit, 183–184
Strawberry Hill Preserve, 21, 187
Stuart, J.E.B., 86, 106–107, 207, 209, 219
Sugarloaf Mountain, 54
Susquehannock Indians, xvii, 54
Swann, Thomas, Jr., 65

Tajitu, 38
Tallyho Theater, 60
Tarara Winery, 79, 118
Tasting Room, 38–39
Taylor, Elizabeth, 209
Taylor, Zachary, 125, 128
Taylor Park, 128, 137
Teddy's Pizza, 210
Temple Hall Farm, 58
Thai Culpeper Restaurant & Bar, 114
Thomas, David, 30
Thomas Balch Library, 53, 65, 180
Thorn Fine Cabinetmakers, 159
Thurmont, 1, 26–30, 174, 192
Tirami Su, 211
Tolbert, John W., 180
Tolliver House, 145
Town Duck, 101
Townsend, George Alfred, 45, 203–204
Trail House, 41
Transient Crafters, 159
Turner, Robert, 202
Turner's Gap, 44, 202
Tuscarora Mill, 68
200 South Street Inn, 159–160

Tyler, John, 155

Underground Railroad, 5, 15, 48, 50, 185
Unison, battle of, 207
University of Virginia, 125–126, 148, 153, 156, 158, 160, 168–171
Upper Crust Bakery, 211
U.S. Route 15, xvii, 1, 3, 54–55, 89, 126, 141–142. *See also* Old Carolina Road

Victoria's Handbag Shop, 159
Vignola Market, 39
Vine Hill, 208
Virginia Company, 101
Virginia Discovery Museum, 161
Virginia Gold Cup, 118
Virginia Room, Fauquier County Library, 95–96
Vivian's, 159

Waddell Memorial Presbyterian Church, 119
Walker, Robert Stringfellow, 127
Walkersville Southern Railroad, 43
Wallace, Lew, 35
Warfield, Wallis, 96
Warren Green Hotel, 90, 96
Warrenton, 89–91, 92–104, 118
Warrenton Cemetery, 98
Washington, George, 108, 168, 198, 209, 215
    Culpeper, 92, 167, 173
    as President, 145–146, 203
Washington & Old Dominion Trail (W&OD), 72, 78, 83
Washington Monument State Park, 45, 203
Waterford, xii, xiv–xv, 78–79, 180, 181–182, 200
West Loudoun Street Café, 68
Westside Café, 39
White's Ferry, 53, 58–59
Whitney State Forest, 103
Wildcat Mountain Natural Area, 104
Wilderness Battlefield, 134, 144, 172–173
William of Orange, 125
Willis, John, 138, 218
Willow Grove Inn, 136, 140
Willowcroft Farm Vineyards, 80
Wills, David, 13, 174
Wilson, Woodrow, 125
Windham Winery, 80, 199
Wolftown, 220
Wolftown Mercantile Country Store, 220
Woodberry School, 127
Wylie Wag, 212

Young, Jacob, 202
Yowell Meadow Park, 119

Zest, 39